Anniversary Edition

Small Steps:

THE YEAR I GOT POLIO

Me at twelve, just before I got polio.

Anniversary Edition

Small Steps:

THE YEAR I GOT POLIO

Peg Kehret

Albert Whitman & Company
Morton Grove, Illinois

Library of Congress Cataloging-in-Publication Data

Kehret, Peg.
Small steps : the year I got polio / written by Peg Kehret.– Anniversary ed.
p. cm.
ISBN 10: 0-8075-7459-7 (hardcover)
ISBN-13: 978-0-8075-7459-1 (hardcover)
1. Kehret, Peg–Health–Juvenile literature.
2. Poliomyelitis–Patients–United States–Biography–Juvenile literature.
I. Title.
RC180.K44 2006
362.196'8350092–dc22
2006005136

The design is by Scott Piehl.
The text of this book is set in Dante and Quadraat.

For information about Albert Whitman & Company,
please visit our web site at www.albertwhitman.com.

For my parents: Beth and Bob Schulze.

Contents

*W*hen I began to write about my polio days, long-forgotten memories bubbled to the surface. I was astonished by the intense emotions these memories brought with them. Those months, more than any other time of my life, molded my personality.

Since I have no transcript of these events, the dialogue is not strictly accurate, but the people mentioned are all real people. The incidents all happened, and the voices are as close to reality as I can make them.

Peg Kehret

1: The Diagnosis

I never thought it would happen to me. Before a polio vaccine was developed, I knew that polio killed or crippled thousands of people, mainly children, each year, but I never expected it to invade *my* body, to paralyze *my* muscles.

Polio is a highly contagious disease. In 1949, there were 42,033 cases reported in the United States. One of those was a twelve-year-old girl in Austin, Minnesota: Peg Schulze. Me.

My ordeal began on a Friday early in September. In school that morning, I glanced at the clock often, eager for the Homecoming parade at four o'clock. As a seventh-grader, it was my first chance to take part in the Homecoming fun. For a week, my friends and I had spent every spare moment working on the seventh-grade float, and we were sure it would win first prize.

SMALL STEPS: THE YEAR I GOT POLIO

My last class before lunch was chorus. I loved to sing, and we were practicing a song whose lyrics are the inscription on the Statue of Liberty. Usually the words "Give me your tired, your poor..." brought goosebumps to my arms, but on Homecoming day, I was distracted by a twitching muscle in my left thigh. As I sang, a section of my blue skirt popped up and down as if jumping beans lived in my leg.

I pressed my hand against my thigh, trying to make the muscle be still, but it leaped and jerked beneath my fingers. I stretched my leg forward and rotated the ankle. *Twitch, twitch.* Next I tightened my leg muscles for a few seconds and then relaxed them. Nothing helped.

The bell rang. When I started toward my locker, my legs buckled as if I had nothing but cotton inside my skin. I collapsed, scattering my books on the floor.

Someone yelled, "Peg fainted," but I knew I had not fainted because my eyes stayed open and I was conscious. I sat on the floor for a moment.

"Are you all right?" my friend Karen asked as she helped me stand up.

"Yes. I don't know what happened."

"You look pale."

"I'm fine," I insisted. "Really."

I put my books in my locker and went home for lunch, as I did every day.

Two days earlier, I'd gotten a sore throat and headache. Now I also felt weak, and my back hurt. What rotten timing, I thought, to get sick on Homecoming day.

Although my legs felt wobbly, I walked the twelve blocks home. I didn't tell my mother about the fall or about my headache and other problems because I knew she would make me stay home.

I was glad to sit down to eat lunch. Maybe, I thought, I should not have stayed up so late the night before. Or maybe I'm just hungry.

When I reached for my milk, my hand shook so hard I couldn't pick up the glass. I grasped it with both hands; they trembled so badly that milk sloshed over the side.

Mother put her hand on my forehead. "You feel hot," she said. "You're going straight to bed."

It was a relief to lie down. I wondered why my back hurt; I hadn't lifted anything heavy. I couldn't imagine why I was so tired, either. I felt as if I had not slept in days.

I fell asleep right away and woke three hours later with a stiff neck. My back hurt even more than before, and now my legs ached as well. Several times I had painful muscle spasms in my legs and toes. The muscles tightened until my knees bent and my toes curled, and I couldn't straighten my legs or toes until the spasms passed.

I looked at the clock; the Homecoming parade started in fifteen minutes.

"I want to go to the parade," I said.

Mother stuck a thermometer in my mouth, said, "One hundred and two," and called the doctor. The seventh-grade float would have to win first place without me. I went back to sleep.

Dr. Wright came, took my temperature, listened to my breathing, and talked with Mother. Mother sponged my forehead with a cold cloth. I dozed, woke, and slept again.

At midnight, I began to vomit. Mother and Dad helped me to the bathroom; we all assumed I had the flu.

Dr. Wright returned before breakfast the next morning and took my temperature again. "Still one hundred and two," he said. He helped me sit up, with my feet dangling over the side of the bed. He tapped my knees with his rubber mallet; this was supposed to make my legs jerk. They didn't. They hung limp and unresponsive.

I was too woozy from pain and fever to care.

He ran his fingernail across the bottom of my foot, from the heel to the toes. It felt awful, but I couldn't pull my foot away. He did the same thing on the other foot, with the same effect. I wished he would leave me alone so I could sleep.

"I need to do a spinal tap on her," he told my parents. "Can you take her to the hospital right away?"

Dad helped me out of bed. I was too sick to get dressed.

At the hospital, I lay on my side while Dr. Wright inserted a needle into my spinal column and withdrew some fluid. Although it didn't take long, it was painful.

The laboratory analyzed the fluid immediately. When Dr. Wright got the results, he asked my parents to go to another room. While I dozed again, he told them the diagnosis, and they returned alone to tell me.

Mother held my hand.

"You have polio," Dad said, as he stroked my hair back from my forehead. "You will need to go to a special hospital for polio patients, in Minneapolis."

Polio! Panic shot through me, and I began to cry. I had seen *Life* magazine pictures of polio patients in wheelchairs or wearing heavy iron leg braces. Each year the March of Dimes, which raised money to aid polio patients and fund research, printed a poster featuring a child in a wheelchair or wearing leg braces or using walking sticks. The posters hung in stores, schools, and libraries—frequent reminders of the terrible and lasting effects of polio. Everyone was afraid of polio. Since the epidemics usually happened in warm weather, children were kept away from swimming pools and other crowded public places every summer because their parents didn't want them exposed to the virus.

How could I have polio? I didn't know anyone who had the disease. Where did the virus come from? How did it get in my body?

I didn't want to have polio; I didn't want to leave my family and go to a hospital one hundred miles away.

As we drove home to pack, I sat slumped in the back seat. "How long will I have to stay in the hospital?" I asked.

"Until you're well," Mother said.

I caught the look of dread and uncertainty that passed between my parents. It might be weeks or months or even years before I came home. It might be never; people sometimes died from polio.

That fear, unspoken, settled over us like a blanket, smothering further conversation.

When we got home, I was not allowed to leave the car, not even to say good-bye to Grandpa, who lived with us, or to B.J., my dog. We could not take a chance of spreading the deadly virus. Our orders were strict: I must contaminate no one.

"Karen called," Mother said when she returned with a suitcase. "The seventh-grade float won second prize." I was too sick and frightened to care.

Grandpa waved at me through the car window. Tears glistened on his cheeks. I had never seen my grandfather cry.

Later that morning, I walked into the isolation ward of the Sheltering Arms Hospital in Minneapolis and went to bed in a private room. No one was allowed in except the doctors and nurses, and they wore masks. My parents stood outside on the grass, waving bravely and blowing kisses through the window. Exhausted, feverish, and scared, I fell asleep.

When I woke up, I was paralyzed.

2: Paralyzed from the Neck Down

My mouth felt full of sawdust; my lips stuck together in the corners. As I opened my eyes, I saw a glass of ice water on the table beside my bed. It was exactly what I needed, but when I tried to reach the water, my right arm did not move.

I tried again. Nothing happened. I tried with my left arm. Nothing. I tried to bend my knees so I could roll on my side, but my legs were two logs, stiff and unmoving. I was too weak even to lift my head off the pillow.

"Help!"

A nurse ran in.

"I can't reach the water," I said. "There's something wrong with my hands. I'm thirsty, but when I try to get the glass..."

"Hush," she said. She lifted the glass and slipped a

straw between my lips. "There you are. Have your drink."

I took only a sip. "What's wrong with my arms and legs?" I asked. "Why can't I move?"

"You have polio," she said, as if that explained everything.

"But I could move before I fell asleep. I walked in here. I had polio then, and I could still move."

"Don't try to talk. Save your energy." She held the straw to my lips again, and I drank the glass of water. "I'll be right back," she said when I finished.

She returned quickly, with a doctor. While he examined me, the nurse held a clipboard and made notes.

"Move your right hand," the doctor said.

I tried; my hand did not move.

"Try to wiggle your fingers."

My fingers lay like an empty glove.

He put his hand around my wrist and lifted my arm a foot off the bed. "Hold your arm in the air when I let go," he said.

I could feel his hand on my wrist, but when he let go, my arm flopped down. I felt like the Raggedy Ann doll I'd left on my bed at home.

He pulled back the sheet. I wore a short hospital gown rather than my own pajamas. I did not remember putting it on, and I wondered who had undressed me.

"Try to lift your left leg."

I closed my eyes and concentrated. My leg remained on the bed.

"Now try to lift your right leg."

My right leg stayed where it was.

"Can you wiggle your toes?"

I could not.

Each time the doctor asked me to move a part of my body and I could not move it, my terror increased. I could talk, I could open and close my eyes, and I could turn my head from side to side on my pillow, but otherwise I could not move at all.

The doctor ran a wooden tongue depressor up the bottoms of my feet. I wanted to kick it away, but my feet wouldn't budge.

He placed his hands on my ribs. "Intercostal expansion is poor," he said.

I felt as if I needed a translator. "What does that mean?" I asked.

"The muscles which expand the rib cage when you breathe are weak," the nurse explained.

The doctor said, "Diagnosis is acute anterior poliomyelitis. The patient is paralyzed from the neck down."

I did not need a translator for his last sentence.

The doctor left, saying he would return in an hour to check me.

"We'll keep you comfortable," the nurse said, "and I'll tell your parents about the paralysis."

"Are they here?" I asked. "I want to see them."

"I'm sorry," she said. "You're in isolation. No visitors are allowed." She started for the door, turned, and added, "We can't risk spreading this disease."

She left me alone with my terror.

Don't think about being paralyzed, I told myself. But how could I think of anything else?

The nurse had forgotten to pull the sheet back up, and the skimpy hospital gown did not even reach my knees. I wanted to cover myself, but I couldn't.

Feeling vulnerable and exposed, I grew more panicky. What if the hospital caught fire? How would I get out?

The doctor's words played over and over in my mind like a broken record. "The patient is paralyzed from the neck down. The patient is paralyzed from the neck down."

I wanted Mother and Dad. I wanted to be well again. I wanted to go home.

When the doctor returned an hour later, I felt short of breath.

"The patient's nostrils are flaring," he said to the nurse. I wondered if he was describing me or a horse.

For two days the fever stayed at one hundred and two, and it became increasingly difficult to breathe. Mostly, I slept, waking often because of muscle spasms or because my back and neck ached so badly. A nurse gently massaged my shoulders, back, and legs, which helped temporarily. I was given aspirin for the pain.

My voice developed a nasal twang. I sounded like a bad tape recording of myself.

The nurses told me that my parents sent their love. They were waiting nearby and wanted to see me, but it was against the hospital rules. I thought the rules were foolish. Mother and Dad had already been exposed to me at home and in the car when they drove me to the hospital, so why couldn't they visit me now?

Doctors and nurses checked me frequently and urged me to drink something. I drank water, but it became harder and harder to swallow. I wanted only to be left alone so I could sleep. When I slept, I did not hurt.

On my third day at the Sheltering Arms, the doctor said, "The patient may need a respirator."

"University Hospital?" the nurse said.

The doctor nodded.

"I'll arrange for an ambulance," the nurse said.

That conversation got my attention, and I roused myself enough to ask, "What's happening?"

The doctor put his hand on my shoulder. "There is more than one kind of polio," he said. "One is spinal polio. It's the most common type and causes paralysis in the patient's arms and legs."

"That's what I have?" I asked. "That's why I can't move?"

"Yes. You have spinal polio. Another kind of polio is respiratory; it causes difficulty in breathing."

I was acutely aware of how hard it was for me to breathe. Was he telling me I had *two* kinds of polio?

"Because you have respiratory polio, too," he said,

"we're transferring you to the University of Minnesota Hospital. We're afraid your lungs may not continue to function on their own."

What was he saying? If my lungs quit working, I would stop breathing, and if I stopped breathing, I would die. Is that what the doctor meant—that I was going to die? I desperately wanted my parents.

The doctor continued: "The Sheltering Arms is a rehabilitation center for polio patients who are trying to regain the use of their muscles. It is not equipped to deal with cases as critical as yours. University Hospital has respirators, and I want you to be near one. If your lungs can't function on their own, the respirator will help. It will breathe for you."

I didn't know what a respirator was, but if it would help me breathe, it must be okay. At least it seemed I was not going to die right on the spot.

"You'll be taken by ambulance to University Hospital," he continued. "I hope you'll be back at the Sheltering Arms soon."

I said nothing. I had not wanted to come to the Sheltering Arms in the first place. Why would I be in any hurry to return?

This move was bad news—it meant I was so sick that I needed a hospital with more emergency facilities than the Sheltering Arms had. I could not sit up. I could not move my arms or legs. It was hard to breathe and I was burning with fever and I was far more frightened than I had ever been in my entire life. I not only had polio, I had two kinds of polio—spinal and respiratory.

"I'll call your parents," the doctor said softly, patting my arm. "They can meet you at University Hospital."

I was transferred from the bed to a gurney and wheeled out a door where an ambulance waited. The cool outdoor air brought me out of my feverish stupor. I was surprised to see that it was dark out; I had lost all track of time.

This is backward, I thought. I walked into the hospital by myself and now, three days later, I can't move at all. Hospitals are supposed to make you get better, not worse.

While the attendants opened the ambulance doors and prepared to load me in, I heard a buzzing sound. A mosquito was flying around my head.

Zzzzt. Zzzzt. I turned my face from side to side, hoping to discourage it from landing on me, but the buzzing grew louder and then abruptly stopped. I could not swat the mosquito or brush it away, and it bit me on the cheek.

As we drove through the streets of Minneapolis, people in cars looked curiously in the ambulance window. I longed to pull the blanket up over my head, but I could not move my hands. Instead, I shut my eyes and pretended I was dead. That seemed a fine joke on those who stared, and gave me great satisfaction.

With my eyes shut, pretending to be dead, I fell asleep. When I woke up, I was in a different hospital bed.

"Where are my parents?" I asked the nurse.

"You're in the isolation ward. No visitors are allowed."

"But the doctor at the Sheltering Arms called them. He told me they would meet me here."

She glanced at my chart. "They were here when you were admitted," she said. "They signed the papers."

"Why didn't someone wake me up?"

Angry tears filled my eyes. I had slept through my chance to see my parents.

No one except the doctors and nurses could come in my room. They wore masks, gowns, and gloves that were sterilized or destroyed after they cared for me.

The next day I had another spinal tap. That afternoon, a new doctor stood beside my bed. "There is more than one kind of polio," he said.

I opened my mouth to interrupt and tell him I already knew all about it, but before I could say anything, he said, "The least common kind is called bulbar polio."

Bulbar? That was a new word. I braced myself for more bad news.

"Bulbar is the most serious form of polio," he continued.

"Worse than spinal or respiratory?" I didn't see how that was possible. What could be worse than being paralyzed from the neck down and unable to breathe properly?

"Bulbar polio impairs the patient's ability to talk or swallow."

I whispered my question. "Do I have bulbar polio?" I knew the answer; why else would he be explaining this? But I had to ask.

His answer was simple and direct. "Yes."

I could think of nothing to say. I had three kinds of polio.

"There's a call button next to your hand," he said,

indicating the cord with a button at the end that lay on my bed. Then he glanced at my chart. "You can't use it, can you?"

I tried to push the button, just in case I'd had a miraculous cure in the last five minutes, but my fingers remained where they were. "No."

"If you can't swallow and start to choke, yell for a nurse. There's always someone nearby."

His words, intended to reassure me, filled me with panic. If I was choking, how could I call for a nurse?

3: An Oxygen Tent and a Chocolate Milkshake

Days and nights blurred together.

My parents came in, wearing hospital gowns, gloves, and masks.

As they stood beside my bed, I saw fear in their eyes. I realized they were allowed into the isolation ward now, when they had not been earlier, because I was so sick that the doctors weren't sure if I would live.

I was glad to have them there, though they were not allowed to touch me and could stay only a few minutes. Always, in the past, they had made everything all right for me. I felt safer knowing they were in the room.

I still had a fever. I ached all over, my throat hurt, and I couldn't shift position in bed without help. Periodically, a nurse turned me from my side to my back and, later, to the other side. That eased the pain temporarily, but it always came back.

"We're going to put you in an oxygen tent," the doctor said. It was the same doctor who had told me about bulbar polio. Was it the same day? The same week? I didn't know if I had slept five minutes or a month.

"We hope the oxygen will keep you breathing on your own," he continued. "If not, a respirator will help you."

I looked where he pointed, and a wave of horror poured over me as I realized *respirator* was another name for what was popularly called an iron lung.

I had seen pictures of people in iron lungs. The tube-shaped machine completely enclosed the patient's body. Only the head stuck out. Bellows pumped air in and out, causing the patient's lungs to expand and contract. Small doors and portholes on the sides of the iron lung allowed the nurses to put their hands in to bathe the patients and help with toileting. Portions of the doors were clear plastic so the nurses could see what they were doing.

Some patients stayed in iron lungs for the rest of their lives, never again breathing by themselves. I thought it would be like being put in a coffin while you were still alive.

Now an iron lung loomed beside my bed, hoses

hanging like tentacles—a gray octopus ready to swallow me at any moment.

As I imagined my future in an iron lung, tears of despair rolled down my cheeks. I could not raise my hand to wipe them away, and they ran into my ears.

Until I got polio, I had led a carefree life. My brother, Art, is six years older than I; my parents had longed for a baby girl, and my birth was cause for celebration. Throughout my childhood, I was dearly loved, and I knew it.

My earliest memories are of swinging, with lilacs in bloom on both sides of my swing—flying high past the purple blossoms, surrounded by the scent; of pushing Raggedy Ann and Marilyn, my favorite dolls, in my doll buggy; of sitting on a picnic bench with my mother's relatives around me, all of them singing, "Sleep, Kentucky Babe" or "You Are My Sunshine."

Nothing in these experiences had prepared me for the words "The patient is paralyzed from the neck down" or the sight of an iron lung standing beside my hospital bed.

The oxygen tent was a sheet of plastic that was draped over me from my waist to the back of my head.

Inside the plastic, oxygen was released for me to breathe. A frame kept the plastic three feet above my head and chest while the four sides hung down to touch my bed. Looking through it was like viewing the room through a foggy windshield.

My parents brought me a teddy bear from Art, who was a freshman at Carleton College. They put the little bear inside the oxygen tent.

"This oxygen tent is just what you need," Mother said, her cheerfulness sounding forced. "It will make it easier to breathe, and you'll soon feel better."

The extra oxygen did ease my breathing, but nothing helped the fever and pain.

Once, in the middle of the night, I awoke aching all over. I badly wanted to roll onto my other side.

"Nurse!" I yelled, as loudly as I could. "Nurse!"

The night nurse rushed into my room.

"I need to be turned," I said.

"What?" She said it as if she had never heard of anything so outrageous.

"I need to be turned," I repeated.

"No, you don't!" She stood beside my bed, hands on her hips, and glared at me.

She was a large woman, and seen through the oxygen tent, she looked even bigger.

"I just turned you, not ten minutes ago," she scolded. "I'm not turning you again already. You'll get turned every thirty minutes, the same as every other patient in this ward."

"But my legs hurt."

"They're going to hurt no matter how many times I roll you around, so you might as well get used to it."

"My back hurts, too. I want to lie on my other side." Years of prodding by my mother surfaced; I added the magic word: "Please?"

"I am too busy to run in here just to turn you in that bed." She shook a finger at me. "Don't you call me again, unless it's an emergency. You hear me? Do not call me unless you can't breathe."

My legs throbbed, my arms ached, my back, neck, and throat hurt. I lay there, helpless, staring at her. She could have turned me in the time it took to tell me no, I thought. And how was I supposed to call for help if I couldn't breathe?

At that moment, I wanted to go home more than I had ever wanted anything, but along with the river of homesickness that flowed through my veins came a trickle of indignation. I was angry at her and angry at my disease. I am not, I decided, going to lie here and be helpless for the rest of my life. I'm going to fight.

I squinted at the nurse through the plastic oxygen tent. Someday, I vowed, she'll be sorry. I'll fight this polio, and I'll beat it. I'll walk out of here, and I'll tell the whole world about the mean nurse who would not help a paralyzed child turn over in bed.

When my parents visited the next day, I told them about the nurse who refused to turn me. They were furious. I don't know what they said, or to whom, but that night, I had a different nurse. The one who wouldn't turn me was never my nurse again.

During those first days in the hospital, I ate almost nothing. Even if food had sounded good, which it didn't, it was now increasingly difficult to swallow. My throat felt swollen shut, and its muscles didn't want to work.

All my life, I had swallowed without any conscious thought. Now I had to think about each step of the process and force my throat muscles to perform what used to be a simple act. It was hard to swallow my own saliva. Food was more than I could manage.

Because of my fever, it was important for me to drink lots of liquid. I tried to drink some ice water each time my parents and the nurses held the glass for me. I was also given apple juice, grape juice, and 7-Up, but they were no easier to swallow than water. I was not offered milk even though I drank milk at home. Because milk creates phlegm, or mucus, in the throat, patients with bulbar polio were not allowed any milk or ice cream for fear it would make them choke.

One evening, a particularly patient nurse coaxed me to drink some 7-Up. She put one hand behind my head and lifted it gently, to make it easier for me to swallow. "Just take little sips," she said.

I wanted to drink the 7-Up, to please her and because I was thirsty. I sucked a mouthful through the straw, but when I tried to swallow, my throat didn't work and all the 7-Up came out my nose. As the fizzy liquid stung the inside of my nose, I sputtered and choked. The choking made it hard to get my breath, and that frightened me. If I couldn't breathe, I would be put in the iron lung.

After that, I didn't want to drink. I was afraid it would come out my nose again; I was afraid of choking. Only the constant urging of my parents and the nurses got enough fluids into me.

Eight days after my polio was diagnosed, my fever still stayed at one hundred two degrees. My breathing was shallow, the painful muscle spasms continued, and every inch of my body hurt. It was like having a bad case of the flu that never ended. My only bits of pleasure in the long hours of pain were the brief visits from my parents and looking at the little teddy bear that Art had sent.

On the afternoon of the eighth day, Mother said, "We can't go on like this. You need more nourishment. You'll never get well if you don't swallow something besides water and juice. Isn't there anything that sounds good? Think hard. If you could have anything you wanted to eat or drink, what would it be?"

"A chocolate milkshake," I said.

NO MILK, my chart stated. NO ICE CREAM.

Mother told a nurse, "Peg would like a chocolate milkshake."

"We can't let her have a milkshake," the nurse replied. "I'm sorry."

"She needs nourishment," Mother declared, "especially liquid. She thinks she can drink a milkshake."

"She could choke on it," the nurse said. "It's absolutely against the doctor's orders." She left the room, muttering about interfering parents.

"You rest for a bit," Mother told me. "We'll be back soon." She and Dad went out.

They returned in less than an hour, carrying a white paper bag. The nurse followed them into my room.

"I won't be responsible for this," she said, as she watched Dad take a milkshake container out of the bag. "Milk and ice cream are the worst things you could give her."

Dad took the lid off the container while Mother unwrapped a paper straw.

"We know you have to follow the rules," Dad said, "but we don't. This is our daughter, and she has had nothing to eat for over a week. If a chocolate milkshake is what she wants, and she thinks she can drink it, then a chocolate milkshake is what she is going to have."

He handed the milkshake to Mother, who put the straw in it.

"What if she chokes to death?" the nurse demanded. "How are you going to feel if you lose her because of a milkshake?"

"If something doesn't change soon," Dad replied, "we're going to lose her anyway. At least this way, we'll know we tried everything we could."

Mother thrust the milkshake under the oxygen tent and guided the straw between my lips.

I sucked the cold, thick chocolate shake into my mouth, held it there for a second, and swallowed. It slipped smoothly down my throat. For the first time since I got sick, something tasted good.

I took another mouthful and swallowed it. I had to work at swallowing, but the milkshake went down. The next mouthful went down, too, and the one after that. I drank the whole milkshake and never choked once, even though I was lying flat on my back the whole time.

When I made a loud slurping sound with my straw because the container was empty, my parents clapped and cheered. The relieved nurse cheered with them.

Within an hour, my temperature dropped. That chocolate milkshake may have saved my life.

4: "You Can't Burn My Bear!"

The next day I swallowed orange juice and broth. Soon I could eat small amounts of soft food such as oatmeal, tapioca pudding, and Jello. My chart still said NO MILK, but any time I asked for a milkshake, I got one.

Within days, I could swallow naturally, without thinking about it, and nothing I drank came back through my nose.

The deep, aching pain went away, and the muscle spasms stopped. It was easier to get my breath, too. The doctors decided to take me out of the oxygen tent for awhile, to see how long I could breathe on my own. My favorite doctor, a young blonde intern named Dr. Bevis, pulled back the plastic tent. I could see around me without everything looking foggy.

Someone turned the crank at the foot of my bed, and the upper half of the bed raised up, putting me in a semi-sitting position. The change felt wonderful.

"Breathe easy," Dr. Bevis said. "Don't take great gulps of air. Relax. Pretend you're going to sleep."

I closed my eyes. Because my chest muscles were so weak, my stomach, rather than my diaphragm, rose and fell as I inhaled and exhaled. Each time my lungs filled with air, my brain filled with excitement. I could breathe without the oxygen tent!

"You're doing great," Dr. Bevis said. "Let's try it on your own. We'll keep the oxygen tent here, in case you need it."

I opened my eyes and grinned at him. "I won't need it," I said.

Later that afternoon, I watched joyfully as the iron lung was rolled out of my room. The next day, the oxygen tent was removed. I had won a major victory; I could breathe by myself.

A nurse gave me more good news: I was moving out of isolation.

"Does that mean I'm not contagious anymore?" I asked.

"That's right. Your parents won't have to put on gowns, masks, and gloves before they visit you." Above her mask, her eyes smiled at me. "And neither will I," she added.

She opened a large bag and began dropping get-well cards into it. I had received dozens of cards and small gifts from family and friends. I had a faint memory of Mother and Dad holding up cards for me to look at through the oxygen tent and telling me who had sent them, but I had been too sick to pay attention.

The window ledge and the bedside table were crowded with cards, stuffed animals, books, and a flowering plant.

As I watched the nurse put a stuffed cat into her bag, I assumed she was moving my belongings to my new ward.

"This afternoon I'm going to have Mother read all my cards to me," I said. "I was so sick when they came that I don't remember who sent them."

"You can't take these cards to your new room," she said.

"Why not? They're mine."

"Anything you had in this room gets burned," she said. Humming cheerfully, she dropped my new books into the bag.

"Burned?" I yelped. "You're going to burn my books? I haven't read them yet. I don't even know the titles."

She fished one of the books out of the bag and read the cover aloud: "*Anne of Green Gables.*"

"I want to read that one. I've heard it's really good."

"I'm sorry," she said. "We have to do this. It's the only way to be sure the virus doesn't spread." Back into the bag went *Anne of Green Gables*, followed by the plant and a box of candy.

"Those are mine!" I shouted, feeling like a two-year-old whose toys were being snatched by a bully. "You can't do that!" I longed to leap from the bed and grab what was rightfully mine out of the nurse's hands.

Just then Mother arrived. I told her what was happening, certain she would make that unfair nurse give me back my belongings.

To my surprise, Mother took the nurse's side. "This has to be done, Peg. The hospital can't let something contagious leave this room."

"But..."

She shook her head firmly, cutting off my protests. "Dad and I knew when we brought your mail to you that this would happen. The nurses told us. We brought it anyway because we hoped that seeing the cards and gifts would help you feel better when you were so sick."

The nurse picked up the teddy bear that Art had sent me.

"Not my bear!" I cried. "You can't burn my bear!"

"I'm sorry," said the nurse as she dropped Teddy into the bag. She sealed the bag with tape, and with gloved hands carried it out of the room.

The teddy bear that had sustained me through the worst week of my life was about to be cremated. I felt like I was murdering my only friend.

"You wouldn't want someone else to get polio just because you kept your teddy bear, would you?" Mother said.

"No," I said. I knew she and the nurse were right, but I still didn't like it one bit. I sulked until I learned that moving out of isolation meant that I could finally wear my own pajamas instead of a hospital gown.

A different bed was wheeled in. After I was lifted onto it, a nurse stripped the sheets and blankets off the old bed and put them in a bag.

"Where do you take the bed, to burn it?" I asked.

"The beds don't get burned. They get sterilized."

"Why couldn't my bear be sterilized? Why do you have to burn him?"

She didn't answer.

I was rolled down the hallway to my new room, which I shared with a little boy in an iron lung. His name was Tommy, and he was eight.

All I could see of Tommy was his head, which stuck out from one end of the iron lung and rested on a canvas strap, much like a small hammock. A mirror over his head allowed him a limited range of vision, but he was unable to see me.

I was glad to have someone besides adults to talk to, but I wished Tommy were closer to my age, and I wished he were a girl. Since I was not able to get out of bed, I had to use a bedpan. I didn't want to do so with a boy in the room.

Tommy told me that lots of people were able to breathe by themselves after being in an iron lung for many months. He was sure this would happen to him, too.

Tommy's iron lung made a soft *swoosh, swoosh* noise as it helped him breathe. I found the sound soothing and went to sleep that night pretending I was in a log cabin on a lake, listening to waves lapping the shore.

In the morning I lay quietly, trying to match my breathing to the rhythmic swooshing of the iron lung. As I did, I welcomed each breath I took, grateful that it could enter my lungs without assistance.

5: Hot Packs

On my first day in the new room, I grumped to Dr. Bevis that the worst part about being paralyzed was that I couldn't paint my toenails. What good, I asked, was a life without painted toenails?

I don't know what made me say such a thing, since I had never painted my toenails before I got sick. Maybe I just wanted handsome Dr. Bevis to notice me.

The next day, Dr. Bevis marched into my room and whisked the covers off my feet. Without saying a word, he took a bottle of bright red nail polish out of his pocket. I was astonished.

"Where did you get nail polish?" I asked.

"I bought it."

"Why?"

"My favorite patient says life is no good without painted toenails." He sat beside me and painted each of my toenails.

I felt like a princess. He had bought nail polish just for

me. *I* was his favorite patient! Instantly, I developed a serious crush on Dr. Bevis.

When he finished, he said, "Now I want you to do something for me."

At that moment, I would have flung myself off the Golden Gate Bridge if he had asked me to.

"What do you want?" I asked, wondering what I could do for him in my condition.

"I want you to get well. Someday, I want to watch you walk." He looked directly into my eyes. "Will you do that for me?"

"Yes."

"Good," he said. "It would make me very happy."

I promised him, and myself, that I would do it. Somehow, some way, I would get well. I would walk for this man who had painted my toenails. For days I insisted that the nurses let my feet stick out from under the blankets so I could admire my beautiful toenails.

Dr. Bevis's visits quickly became the highlights of every day. I tried to remember every knock, knock joke I'd ever heard so that I would have something to tell him. I wanted to make him laugh, and I also hoped to make him stay in my room longer.

When I couldn't remember any more knock, knock jokes, I began to make them up. I spent hours thinking of puns and figuring out ways to use them. My favorite was:

"Knock, knock."

"Who's there?"

"Wendy."

"Wendy who?"

"Wendy toenails are painted, de patient gets well."

Dr. Bevis groaned, but I could tell he liked it. Tommy liked it, too.

I asked my parents for a radio because I missed hearing my favorite program, the "Lone Ranger." They bought a small portable radio, and at six-thirty that night, I asked one of the nurses to tune in the "Lone Ranger" for me. As soon as the familiar theme song began, Tommy let out a whoop of glee.

"Oh, boy!" he cried. "We get to hear the 'Lone Ranger'!" He said he used to listen to every broadcast before he got sick.

The nurse placed the radio between my bed and Tommy's iron lung so we could both hear. When our hero called to his horse, "Hi-yo, Silver! Awa-a-ay!" Tommy and I yelled, too. From then on, I called Tommy

Tonto, the name of the Lone Ranger's companion, and he called me kemo sabe, which means faithful friend. We sometimes listened to music, too, or the "Archie Andrews" show, but we could hardly wait for six-thirty on Mondays, Wednesdays, and Fridays so we could hear the "Lone Ranger." It felt good to have something to look forward to again.

We could not look forward to a fast recovery, for there was no medicine for polio. The doctors hoped to minimize its effects, however, with the Sister Kenny treatments. These treatments, named for Sister Elizabeth Kenny, the Australian nurse who first used them, consisted of two parts. The first was hot packs, and I had begun getting these twice a day in isolation, as soon as my fever broke.

For this part of the treatment, I lay on my stomach, dressed only in underpants. Because my shoulder muscles were so weak, a rolled-up towel was put under each shoulder to keep them from becoming too rounded.

Then a nurse wheeled a big metal tank filled with steaming water up to my bed. The wheels squeaked and rattled across the floor as she approached, sounding like a freight train approaching its station. She put large gray woolen cloths in the hot water and then lifted them out with tongs so she wouldn't burn her fingers. She flattened the cloths in a wringer attached to the side of the tank, removing most of the moisture. The steam from the cloths filled my nostrils; I grew to dread the smell of wet wool.

As the hot cloths came out of the wringer, the nurse laid them across my bare back and the backs of my legs and arms.

The first time I had a hot packs treatment, I thought the nurse had made a mistake and heated the water too high. It felt like the hot packs were burning all my skin off. I screamed and cried, even though the nurse assured me that I wasn't being scalded. She said the water had to be that hot in order to help me.

After a few minutes, as the hot packs began to cool, they felt good because the warm, moist heat helped my tight muscles relax.

When the cloths cooled to lukewarm, they were removed, and a fresh batch of hot packs was laid across my back, arms, and legs. This went on for an hour, with the nurse taking the steaming cloths from the hot water, wringing them out, and plunking them on my bare skin.

Each time a cool cloth was removed, I closed my eyes and braced myself for the first searing moments of the next hot one. The backs of my thighs were particularly tender, and every time a hot pack was laid there, I was sure my skin was being blistered and burned.

On my second day of treatment, I asked, "How many more times do I have to get hot packs?" I thought the hot packs were like medicine—take two times a day for seven days, and then it would be over.

"Oh, the hot packs continue as long as you're here," the nurse said as she plucked another steaming cloth from the boiling water.

That could be weeks, I thought. Months, even.

"Of course," she continued, "hot packs are only one part of the Kenny treatment. As soon as you're out of isolation, you'll get the second part."

6: Torture Time

"Stop!" I cried. "It hurts!"

Part two consisted of special exercises. During the acute stage of polio, when the patient has a fever, frequent spasms tighten the muscles. Those muscles must be gradually stretched back to normal before they can regain strength.

After I was moved out of isolation, I had my first physical therapy session. Immediately after my morning hot packs treatment, a physical therapist turned me onto my back. She grasped my right ankle with one hand, put her other hand on my right knee to keep my leg straight, and raised my leg until it was straight up from my stomach.

Because the big hamstring muscles in the backs of my legs were so tight, it was painful to hold my leg in that position, even after the hot packs.

I begged the therapist to stop, but she held my leg

firmly upright. "I'm only trying to help you get well," she said.

At last, she put my leg down—and immediately grasped the other leg and stretched it. I couldn't kick or pull away from her hands. My mouth was my only defense, and I used it, shrieking and crying.

"Stop that," she snapped. "You should be ashamed, making such a scene."

I stopped yelling, but I wasn't ashamed, and I couldn't control the tears that streamed down my cheeks.

"This is even worse than the hot packs," I complained when she finally put my leg down. "At least the hot packs feel good part of the time, after they cool off a little. The stretching exercises hurt all the time."

"Be grateful you are here at all," the therapist told me.

After she left, I told Tommy her name was Mrs. Crab. From then on, that is what we called her.

"Mrs. Crab never had polio," I said. "She doesn't know how much it hurts."

That afternoon, Mrs. Crab came again. I groaned and said, "It's Torture Time."

Tommy giggled and repeated my comment to all of his nurses.

From then on, my muscles were stretched twice a day. Another exercise that I hated was one that stretched my hamstrings and my back at the same time. For this one, I was pushed up until I sat upright in bed, with my legs out in front of me. The bottoms of both feet were placed flat against a board at the foot of the bed. Then Mrs. Crab put her hand on the back of my head, held my chin to my chest, and pushed my head down toward my knees.

The pain began at the back of my neck and ran all the way down my spine and along the backs of both legs. Each time Mrs. Crab pushed, I thought I could not bear it. Then she pushed harder.

No one ever explained the purpose of these stretching exercises to me. Mrs. Crab said, "This will help you get well," but I didn't understand how, and I wasn't willing to take her word for it. All I knew was that twice every day my body was forced to move in ways that hurt.

Each time Mrs. Crab pushed my head toward my knees, I groaned louder. The more I complained, the more she belittled me.

"You're acting like a baby," she said, "instead of a big girl, twelve years old. Look at little Tommy, lying there in an iron lung. You don't hear him crying."

"You aren't stretching his hamstrings," I said. "He's perfectly comfortable."

"You should be glad you're well enough to get therapy," she replied. "You should thank me, instead of crying all the time."

"Thank you for torturing me," I said.

She pushed my head down an extra inch. I was sure my spinal cord would snap in two if she leaned any harder.

Perhaps Mrs. Crab expected me to act more mature because I was tall for my age. At twelve, I had already reached my full adult height of five feet, eight inches.

But I had led a sheltered life in a small Midwestern town. Television was not yet common, and the only movies I had seen were *Bambi* and half of *Snow White*. (My parents had to take me out in the middle of *Snow White* because I was so frightened of the witch.) Except for having my tonsils out, I had never been away from my parents overnight. Because my grandpa lived with us, I had never even stayed with a babysitter. Now I was far from home, in pain, and scared.

Dad had to go back to work, and since visiting hours (Sundays only) were enforced after I was out of isolation,

Mother went home with him. Austin was one hundred miles from the hospital in Minneapolis. Mother and Dad planned to visit me each Sunday, but they were no longer my daily support system. I was on my own in dealing with Mrs. Crab.

By then, I knew that my chances of moving normally again were slim. I remembered the stories about polio epidemics that I had heard before I got sick; I recalled the pictures of polio patients in wheelchairs and leg braces. At least they could use their arms and hands; I couldn't even do that.

When I asked the nurses questions about my future, their answers were vague. "Each case is different," one told me. "We can't know for sure what will happen."

Although nobody came right out and said I would not get better, I sensed that the staff had seen many patients in my condition who remained paralyzed, and this terri-fied me. My parents and Dr. Bevis stayed optimistic, but I suspected they were only trying to keep me from panicking.

Part of every day was taken up with routine care. Dr. Bevis checked me twice a day. Hot packs and stretching exercises lasted an hour and a half each morning and again each afternoon. My sheets were changed daily, and the nurses took my temperature regularly. I was fed, turned, and bathed.

Still, the days seemed endless. I had plenty of time to lie there and worry. I thought about my school, which was a three-story building that had no ramps or elevators, only stairs. How could I finish school in a wheelchair?

What will happen to me? I wondered. I loved animals and books; I wanted to be either a veterinarian or a writer, but either profession now seemed beyond reach.

I thought about how our family veterinarian lifted B.J. onto the examining table for his checkups. It seemed unlikely that I would ever be able to lift so much as a pet mouse.

Writers must be able to hold a pencil or use a typewriter, and I could do neither. Even the ordinary hope of being a wife and mother someday was dim; who would want to marry a woman who couldn't go to the bathroom alone? My future seemed bleak, and yelling through Torture Time was a way to vent my frustration.

I knew, when I screamed and cried, that I was being difficult. I even realized that Mrs. Crab would not be so hard on me if I cooperated, but I felt she was wrong to make light of my pain, and so I continued to carry on.

One morning, Dr. Bevis came along while I was having my Torture Time. As usual, I shouted and moaned while Mrs. Crab told me what a crybaby I was. Dr. Bevis stood beside my bed for a moment, watching. Suddenly embarrassed at my own behavior, I stopped yelling. I didn't want my hero to see me at my worst.

"It hurts, doesn't it?" he said.

I nodded.

"If you do these exercises," he said, "one of these days you'll walk for me. If you don't do them . . ." He shrugged and let me figure out the consequences myself.

I swallowed a scream as Mrs. Crab forced my head toward my knees.

"I'm proud of you for working so hard," Dr. Bevis said.

"Hmpf," sniffed Mrs. Crab.

That's all he said. That's all he needed to say. His words of acceptance and encouragement changed my behavior far more effectively than the therapist's constant scolding.

With all my heart, I longed to keep my promise to walk for Dr. Bevis. I wanted it not only to please him;

I wanted it for myself. If I had to stretch my muscles in order to walk again, then I would stretch my muscles, no matter how much it hurt.

But I still didn't like Mrs. Crab. And whenever I was sure Dr. Bevis was not nearby, I still yelled.

7: Star Patient Surprises Everyone

On October first, I lay in bed with my eyes closed, rehearsing a new joke. As I imagined Dr. Bevis's laughter, my leg itched. Without thinking, I scratched the itch. Then, as I realized what I had done, my eyes sprang open.

Had I really used my hand? After three weeks of paralysis, I was almost afraid to believe it, for fear I had dreamed or imagined the movement. Holding my breath, I tried again. The fingers on my left hand moved back and forth.

"I CAN MOVE MY HAND!!" I yelled.

Two nurses rushed into the room.

"Look! I can move my left hand!" I wiggled my fingers jubilantly.

"Get Dr. Bevis," said one of the nurses. She smiled at me as the other nurse hurried out of the room.

"Can she really do it?" asked Tommy. "Can she move her hand?"

"Yes," said the nurse. "Her fingers are moving."

"Hooray!" shrieked Tommy. "The Lone Ranger rides again!"

Dr. Bevis came bounding in. "What is all this shouting about?"

Feeling triumphant, I moved my fingers.

"Try to turn your hand over," he said.

I tried. The hand didn't go all the way, but it moved. It definitely moved. It was Christmas and my birthday and the Fourth of July, all at the same time. I could move my hand!

Dr. Bevis turned my hand palm up. "Try to bend your arm," he said.

My hand lifted an inch or so off the bed before it dropped back down.

"What about the other hand?" he asked. "Is there any movement in your right hand?"

To my complete astonishment, my right hand moved, too. Bending at the elbow, my lower arm raised several inches and I waved my fingers at Dr. Bevis.

By then, I was so excited I felt as if I could jump from that bed and run laps around the hospital.

"This is wonderful," Dr. Bevis said. "This is terrific!"

I agreed.

"When your mother makes her daily phone call," Dr. Bevis said, "she is going to be thrilled."

In the next few days, I improved rapidly. Soon I could use both hands, then my arms. I was able to sit up, starting with two minutes and working up to half an hour. Movement returned to my legs, too. My arms were still extremely weak, but I learned to feed myself again, which did wonders for both my attitude and my appetite. I was no longer totally helpless.

With my bed cranked up, I could balance a book on my stomach and turn the pages myself. I had always liked to read, and now books provided hours of entertainment. The hospital had a small library; day after day, I lost myself in books.

I began reading aloud to Tommy. I quit only when my voice got hoarse, but even then he always begged me to read just one more page. I preferred reading silently because it was faster, but I felt sorry for Tommy who was still stuck in the iron lung, unable to hold a book. I was clearly getting better; he was not. Each day, I read to him until my voice gave out.

Dr. Bevis continued to praise and encourage me. Mrs. Crab bragged about my progress. The nurses called me their star patient. I realized that no one had thought I would ever regain the use of my arms and legs.

A week after I first moved my hand, Dr. Bevis said he wanted to see if I could stand by myself. First, he helped me sit on the edge of the bed. Then, with a nurse on each side, I was eased off the bed until my feet touched the floor. Each nurse had a hand firmly under one of my armpits, holding me up.

"Lock your knees," Dr. Bevis instructed. "Stand up straight."

I tried to do as he said.

"We're going to let go," he said, "but we won't let you fall. When the nurses drop their arms, see if you can stand by yourself."

Tommy, my iron lung cheerleader, hollered, "Do it, kemo sabe! Do it!"

It was wonderful to feel myself in an upright position again. I was sure I would be able to stand alone. I even imagined taking a step or two.

"All right," Dr. Bevis said to the nurses. "Let go."

As soon as they released me, I toppled. Without support, my legs were like cooked spaghetti. The nurses and Dr. Bevis all grabbed me to keep me from crashing to the floor.

Disappointment filled me, and I could tell the others were disappointed, too. The strength had returned so quickly to my arms and hands that everyone expected my legs to be better also.

"I'm sorry," I said. "I tried."

"It will happen," Dr. Bevis said.

They helped me back into bed, and I was grateful to lie down again. Standing for that short time, even with help, had exhausted me and made my back ache.

The twice-daily hot packs and stretching continued, and so did my progress. Each small achievement, such as being able to wiggle the toes on one foot, was heralded with great joy. I had to keep my feet flat against a board at the foot of my bed to prevent them from drooping forward permanently, and I longed to lie in bed without that board.

Although I was delighted with every small accomplishment, I wondered why I got better and some of the other patients did not. Tommy might spend the rest of his life in the iron lung. It didn't seem fair.

I mentioned this to Dr. Bevis. "Some cases of polio are severe, and some are mild," he said. "When the polio virus completely destroys a nerve center, the muscles controlled by that center are paralyzed forever. If the damage is slight rather than total, the paralysis is temporary. Your muscles were severely weakened, but the nerve damage wasn't total. It's possible for weak muscles to gain back some of their strength."

"So Tommy's polio is worse than mine," I said.

"That's right. It also helped that your parents took you to the doctor right away. You were already here and diagnosed when you needed oxygen; some people who have respiratory polio are not that fortunate."

I remembered how hard it had been to breathe, and how much the oxygen tent had helped.

Dr. Bevis continued, "Most people think they have the flu and don't get medical help until paralysis sets in. By the time they learn they have polio, and get to a hospital that's equipped to treat them, the respiratory patients often have to go straight into an iron lung. They don't get hot packs or physical therapy until they can breathe on their own again, which might be several months later. The sooner the Sister Kenny treatments are started, the more they help." He smiled at me. "You are one lucky girl."

But it wasn't all luck, I thought; it was quick action by my parents. They helped create my good luck.

"I've been wondering something else, too," I said. "How did I get polio when not one other person in my town got it?"

"Many people have polio and never know it," Dr. Bevis said. "They are highly contagious, but because their symptoms are so slight, they don't see a doctor. There are probably thousands of cases of polio every year that are so mild they are never diagnosed."

"So I caught it from someone who didn't know they had it," I said. It seemed unbelievable to me that anyone could have polio and not realize it.

Mail was delivered every afternoon, and I looked forward to a daily letter from my mother. Most of her letters were signed, "Love, Mother and Dad," but a few were signed with a muddy paw print. Those were from B.J., telling me he had chased a cat or buried a bone. Grandpa depended on Mother to tell me any news, but he sent a gift each week when my parents came to visit.

Art wrote about college life and sent me a new teddy bear just like the one that got burned.

One mail delivery included a big brown packet from my school in Austin. When I opened it, dozens of letters from my classmates tumbled out. Karen wrote about a student petition to change the rules so girls could wear pants to school instead of the required dresses. Another girl complained that her new haircut was too short; a third was outraged at the basketball referee.

I had the strange feeling that I was reading about a different lifetime. The other kids were upset about such unimportant things.

Just a few weeks earlier, I, too, had worried about clothes and hair and the basketball team. Now none of this mattered. I had faced death. I had lived with excruciating pain and with loneliness and uncertainty about the future. Bad haircuts and lost ball games would never bother me again.

Even the petition to allow girls to wear pants to school, a cause I supported, failed to excite me. I would happily wear a gunnysack, I thought, if I could walk into the school.

"Be glad you aren't here," one boy wrote. "You aren't missing anything but hard tests and too much home-work."

He's wrong, I thought. I miss my own room and playing with B.J. and helping Grandpa in the garden. I miss my piano lessons and roller-skating and licking the pan when Mother makes fudge. I miss visiting my aunts and uncles. I miss riding my bike with Karen and playing Monopoly with Richard.

I put the letters aside, knowing I was changed forever. My world was now the hospital. Would I have anything in common with my classmates when I went home? I felt closer now to Tommy, whose head was the only part of him I had ever seen, than I did to the kids who used to be my dearest friends. Tommy understood what it was like to have polio; my school friends could never know.

8: Roommates

In mid-October, Dr. Bevis told me, "I have wonderful news. You're being discharged from University Hospital and going back to Sheltering Arms for rehabilitation."

I burst into tears. "That isn't wonderful! I don't want to leave; I want to stay here!"

Dr. Bevis patted my shoulder. "We've done all we can for you here," he said. "You need different therapy now. You'll have a new doctor and—"

"I don't want a new doctor. I want you."

"—and a new physical therapist."

Tommy said, "No more Mrs. Crab."

I blew my nose. "Do I have to?" I asked. "Can't I be rehabilitated here?"

"We don't do it here. We handle only acute cases."

"Tommy's been here longer than I have, and you aren't kicking him out," I said.

"Tommy still needs the respirator."

"I don't know anybody at the Sheltering Arms."

"You didn't know anyone here when you first came. It's always hard to be the new kid, but you'll adjust."

I saw there was no use arguing.

"When do I leave?" I asked.

"This afternoon. The discharge papers are all ready. Actually, they were ready a couple of days ago, but the Sheltering Arms didn't have a bed for you until now."

"You've known for two days that I was leaving? Why didn't anyone tell me?"

"Maybe we were afraid you'd make a fuss."

I scowled at him, aware that I was making a fuss.

"They probably won't even paint my toenails," I said.

He laughed and went out the door.

This time I could take my belongings with me. My clothes, books, and the new teddy bear were packed in a paper bag.

All morning, nurses stopped by to wish me well. Even Mrs. Crab came to say good-bye. "I know you hated the exercises because they hurt," she said, "but someday you'll thank me for making you do them."

I doubted it.

"I'll miss you," Tommy said, "especially your reading to me and your knock, knock jokes. And I'll miss the 'Lone Ranger.'"

"You can keep my radio," I told him. "Think about me every Monday, Wednesday, and Friday."

"No kidding? I get to keep the radio?"

"Sure. My parents can bring me my radio from home."

That wasn't true. I didn't have my own radio at home; I listened to the "Lone Ranger" on our family radio. But in the time we had been together, no one had visited Tommy, for his family lived hundreds of miles away. They probably didn't know that he wanted a radio at the hospital. I decided Tommy needed to hear the "Lone Ranger" more than I did.

"Thanks," he said. "I hope you learn to walk again."

I looked at his small head, protruding from the iron lung. The soft *swoosh, swoosh* of the machine had been background music for our reading, for every conversation, and for the "Lone Ranger" broadcasts. Now I was being released, while my fellow inmate in the prison of paralysis might listen to the swooshing forever.

"I hope you learn to breathe without the respirator," I told him, and I had never made a more sincere wish. "Good-bye, Tonto."

"Adios, kemo sabe."

As I was being transferred to the ambulance gurney, Dr. Bevis pinned a yellow rose to my pajama top. "For my favorite patient," he said.

My lip began to tremble.

He said, "Knock, knock."

I blinked back my tears. "Who's there?"

"Yul."

"Yul, who?"

"Yul be back soon, to walk for me."

"That's right," I said, as I was lifted into the ambulance.

At the Sheltering Arms, I was put in a large room with four other girls. Instead of the sterile white walls and white blankets that I'd had at University Hospital, Room 202 was full of color, with striped blankets, flowered curtains, and pictures on the walls. There was even a bookcase filled with books.

We each had a hospital bed that could be cranked up so that our heads and shoulders were elevated. This allowed us to see each other, and I quickly became acquainted with my new roommates.

Dorothy was fourteen, a cheerful girl with a shy, sweet smile. She was sitting in a wheelchair when I arrived, and she waved a welcome. I liked her immediately.

"I came here from University Hospital, too," she said, "on my birthday. I was still paralyzed then, from the neck down."

Dorothy told me she had been at the Sheltering Arms for two months and was hoping to learn to walk with braces on her legs.

Shirley, who was also fourteen, was fighting a double problem. She had been born with arms that only straightened halfway. Now polio had made her situation worse. After seven months in the hospital, she still had no movement in her legs. Because of back weakness, she could sit in a wheelchair for only brief periods. She also had breathing problems.

Renée, petite and dark-haired, was twelve, like me. "I'm learning to walk with leg braces and walking sticks," she told me. "I'll probably always have to use them, unless physical therapy works wonders."

At the mention of physical therapy, I groaned. "I call physical therapy Torture Time," I said.

"It isn't so bad," Renée said. "At least I'm out of the iron lung."

"You were in an iron lung?" I said.

Renée nodded. "At University Hospital. I was in one for five months."

"I was in an iron lung, too," said Shirley.

"So was I," said Dorothy.

My hopes for Tommy soared. Maybe he would get out of the iron lung.

I looked at the last of my roommates, who also was in a wheelchair. She hadn't said anything.

"This is Alice," Dorothy said. "She's thirteen."

Alice was a sturdy-looking girl with wide eyes and soft curls. Her toes pointed permanently downward, the "dropfoot" condition that the footboard on my hospital bed was intended to prevent. I asked her how long she had been at the Sheltering Arms.

"Ten years," she said.

I gaped at her. "Ten *years*? You've been here since you were three years old?"

"Well, well," Alice said. "The genius can subtract."

"When will you be able to go home?" I asked.

"I *am* home."

"Alice lives at Sheltering Arms," Renée said.

Disbelieving, I pressed on. "But what about your parents? Don't you have any family?"

"My parents," said Alice, "don't want me."

I stared at her, not knowing what to say.

"After I'd been here a few months, the doctors said I could go home, but I would never get any better," Alice said.

I waited.

"My parents refused to take me. They didn't want a big old crippled-up blob on their hands for the rest of their lives."

I realized she wanted to shock me, and she succeeded. I was speechless.

Renée continued the explanation. "Alice comes from a big family," she said. "She got polio before the doctors knew about hot packs and muscle stretches. When she didn't get well, her parents were unable to take care of her and all of the other kids, too, so she became a ward of the state."

"I—I'm sorry," I said.

"Don't feel sorry for me!" Alice snapped. "I like it here. I wouldn't leave if they paid me."

I thought about my own parents. I knew they would never refuse to take me home, no matter what condition I was in. For the first time since my paralysis set in, I realized there was something worse than having polio.

"Don't look so horrified," Alice said. "Dorothy could go home, too, if there was someone to take care of her."

I looked nervously across the room. Had another of my roommates been abandoned by her family?

Dorothy smiled reassuringly. "I live on a farm," she said, "and everyone has to work. I can't go home until I can get around by myself because once I'm home, there won't always be someone to help me. My family can't afford to hire help. I'm learning to put braces on my legs now, so it shouldn't be too much longer."

"You hope," said Alice. The chip on her shoulder seemed the size of a fireplace log, but I didn't blame her for being mad at the world.

I had never thought of myself as a privileged child. My dad sold meat for the Hormel Company. My mother was a homemaker. Grandpa worked in a print shop, setting type. Ours was an average middle-class family.

Now I saw how lucky I was, not only to have parents who loved me, but parents who were able to care for me and to meet my needs, whatever they might be. I had absolutely no doubt that if the doctors said I could go home, I would be out the door the next day.

And if I ended up a big old crippled-up blob, as Alice put it? I shuddered. Even though I knew my parents would always love me and take care of me, I didn't want them to *have* to. I wanted to go home and return to school and be a normal person. And I wanted to go back to University Hospital and walk for Dr. Bevis.

I was going to meet my new physical therapist, Miss Ballard, the next morning and I dreaded it. What if she was another Mrs. Crab? Or worse?

After hearing Alice's story, I decided I would do everything Miss Ballard asked me to do, even if she was the torture champion of all time.

9: Sunday Visitors

Miss Ballard was young and pretty, with a friendly smile, but I was wary as I answered her questions about myself. "I'm going to watch you do some exercises," she said, "so I'll know best how to help you."

Here it comes, I thought, more Torture Time.

To my surprise, each time Miss Ballard asked me to move an arm or leg, she said, "Please." When I did as she asked, she said, "That's good. You're doing great." I did arm and hand movements, followed by leg and foot movements. Each time, Miss Ballard praised my efforts, even when I was not able to do everything that she asked me to do.

"Just one more," she said. She sat me up in bed, with my feet flat against the footboard, and put her hand on the back of my head.

She saved the worst for last, I thought, remembering how it hurt my back and hamstring muscles when Mrs.

Crab shoved my head toward my knees. I shut my eyes, determined not to cry out in front of my roommates.

"Let me know when this starts to hurt," she said. "I want to stretch your muscles and keep them loose, but I don't ever want you to feel real pain."

My eyes popped open. "You don't?" I said.

"Of course not."

I could hardly believe my ears.

Miss Ballard pushed slowly, applying gentle, steady pressure. Even when it began to hurt, I didn't tell her right away. Knowing she would stop when I asked her to, I let her push a tiny bit farther. From then on, I always let her go a little beyond the point where it hurt, so I would get well that much faster.

Miss Ballard was lavish with praise for my efforts. She even listened to my knock, knock jokes. Soon I looked forward to my daily physical therapy sessions.

I got a wheelchair and was allowed to sit up for an hour at a time. I was especially glad that I could be wheeled to the bathroom, instead of using a bedpan.

I called my wheelchair my iron horse, and like the Lone Ranger, I named my horse Silver. Each time I got into the wheelchair, I yelled, "Hi, yo, Silver! Awa-a-ay!"

and whacked the side with the palm of my hand.

The Sheltering Arms allowed visitors twice a week: on Wednesday evenings and on Sundays from noon until four. My home in Austin was a two-hour drive, so Wednesday evenings were out of the question for my parents.

The first Sunday, I could hardly wait for twelve o'clock. I combed my hair twice and gobbled my lunch. "My parents are coming today," I told the nurse as I handed her my lunch tray.

"You hope," said Alice.

"They'll be here," I said. "It's Sunday."

"It's sleeting," Alice pointed out. "The roads will be terrible."

From my bed, I peered anxiously out the window at the icy rain. Alice was right; the roads were probably slick. But surely, I thought, Mother and Dad would call if they were not coming, so I wouldn't worry about them.

"They'll be here," I repeated, trying to convince myself as well as Alice.

Promptly at noon, Mother and Dad swept in the door, their arms full of bags and packages.

"What a nice, bright room," Mother said. "And you

have roommates your own age. How wonderful!"

The introductions were made, and then I opened the packages. There were extra pajamas, more books, and a box of stationery with the envelopes already stamped.

"Potato chips!" I shouted.

"The hospital never serves potato chips," said Renée.

Dad pried open the can, and I began to munch. Mother passed the can to the other girls.

Even more welcome than potato chips was news from home. The Usems had a new car; Mrs. Meany had opened an antiques shop; Steve Gentle was taking piano lessons. I listened eagerly—and so did Dorothy, Renée, Shirley, and Alice.

Midway through the afternoon, it began to irritate me that I wasn't able to talk alone with my parents. If Dad said something funny, everyone laughed. Why did my roommates have to listen to every word? Didn't they know it wasn't polite to eavesdrop on other people's conversation?

The moment I asked myself the question, I knew the answer. I was the only one who had visitors. I had assumed that all of the girls would have company on Sunday—except for Alice, of course.

Apparently, Mother had the same thought because she turned to the other girls and asked, "Are any of you expecting visitors?"

"It's too far for my family to come," Shirley said. "They've only been here twice." Twice! In seven months!

"My parents try to come once a month," Dorothy said, "but it depends on whether they can get someone to do chores for them."

"What about you?" Mother asked Renée. "Will you be having visitors today?"

Renée shook her head. "I live more than two hundred miles away," she said. "My parents would like to come every week, but it isn't possible." Then, as if to prove that her family did not neglect her, she added, "They write to me, though. I get a lot of mail."

Last, Mother turned to Alice. Don't ask, I thought, but of course Mother did.

"I don't get company," Alice said.

"Not ever?" Dad said.

"One of my brothers came once, but when he saw how ugly I am, he never came back."

"You aren't ugly," Dad said. "You're pretty."

"Ha!" said Alice.

"We'll visit all of you next Sunday," Mother said. "And we'll bring treats for everyone."

"What would you like?" Dad asked. "Renée? What should we bring for you?"

After some thought, Renée asked for a comic book. "*Little Lulu*," she said, "or *Archie and Veronica*."

"Shirley?" Mother said. "What can we bring for you?"

Shirley replied instantly. "A bag of marshmallows."

"Plain old marshmallows?" Dad asked.

"I love marshmallows," Shirley said. "The big, puffy kind."

Dorothy could not decide.

"I know what she really wants," Renée said. "A tall, dark, and handsome young man."

While the rest of us laughed, Dorothy pulled the covers over her head. When we quit laughing, she said, "Do you think I could have some licorice?"

Alice refused to ask for a special treat.

"There must be something you'd like us to bring you," Dad said. "Something you can't get here at the Sheltering Arms."

Alice shook her head. At first I thought she was being ornery; then I realized Alice had been at the Sheltering

Arms for so long she didn't remember things like comic books and marshmallows. Licorice and potato chips were beyond her realm of experience. She didn't know what to ask for because she did not know what she was missing.

A window of understanding opened in my mind, and the breeze of compassion blew in. From that moment on, I was glad to share my visiting family with my room-mates.

"If you don't know what you want," Mother told Alice, "we'll surprise you."

The next Sunday, the other girls were as excited about visiting day as I was. Alice combed her hair, though she quit when she saw me watching her.

Once again, Mother and Dad came in right at twelve o'clock. They hugged and kissed me and greeted all the other girls.

"Did you remember our treats?" Renée asked.

"Of course," Mother said. She handed Renée a *Little Lulu* comic book. Dad opened Shirley's bag of marshmallows and put one in her mouth.

"Yum," Shirley said. "That's the first marshmallow I've had for seven months."

"Here is your gift, Alice," Mother said as she gave Alice a pink lipstick.

"Why are you being so nice to me?" Alice asked.

"We like you," Mother said.

Alice didn't say thank you, but she put the lipstick carefully away in her drawer.

"Dorothy's next," Renée said. "Where's her tall, dark, and handsome young man?"

Dad went to the doorway and motioned to someone in the hall.

In walked my brother, Art. Art was eighteen and six feet, two inches tall, with thick, dark hair. He was once voted Campus Dreamboat by a sorority group.

After Art hugged me, he said, "I didn't come to visit you. I came to see Dorothy. Which one is Dorothy?"

Dorothy blushed red as a wagon while the rest of us squealed our delight.

"This is for you," Art said, and he gave Dorothy a bag of licorice.

Every Sunday after that, all of us chattered happily as we waited for my parents to arrive. Each Sunday at four, I hated to see them leave. The afternoons together were such fun, and it would be a whole week until I saw them again.

But when I started to feel sorry for myself, I looked across the room at Alice. I only had to wait one week before my parents returned. Hers were never coming.

10: Happy
Thirteenth Birthday

On the first Sunday in November, Dad said, "Next week, we're going to have a birthday party." He turned to me. "Or did you forget what day is coming?"

Every year since I was old enough to know the date, I had counted the days until it was time for presents and a party. This year, I had completely forgotten. Without school events to keep track of, and Mother's "Daily Reminder Calendar" next to the telephone, my days and weeks ran together like cream in coffee.

"By this time next week," Mother said, "we'll have another teenager in the family."

"A grown-up, mature young woman," said Dad.

"Ha!" said Alice.

A teenager. I was going to be thirteen years old. I wondered what awaited me in the year to come. A wheelchair of my own? Braces on my legs? Walking sticks? Or perhaps during my thirteenth year I would learn to walk. Perhaps I would go home.

Home. What a powerful word. It caused pictures to flash through my mind like slides fast-forwarding on a screen.

Home was a three-story yellow house with a large kitchen where we ate most of our meals, a dining room for special occasions, and a living room that contained, among other things, the piano where I practiced my lessons.

My bedroom was upstairs, and in my mind, I entered it gladly. I saw my bed, my four-drawer dresser, the rug on the floor, even my messy closet, which Mother always nagged me to clean out so I wouldn't attract spiders.

I loved every inch of that house, but home was more than walls and furniture. It was Grandpa sitting beside me at dinner and B.J. at my feet, hoping for a handout. It was Mother singing in the kitchen and the smell of freshly laundered sheets that had dried in the sun.

Home was Dad arriving at six o'clock, bringing me a piece of bubble gum; home was macaroni and cheese for supper; home was feeling safe and cherished.

"Are we really going to have a party?" Dorothy asked.

"Right here in this room," Dad said, "and it's going to be a wing-dinger."

"I've never been to a birthday party," Alice said.

"We'll fix that," said Mother.

It was easier to have them leave at four o'clock, knowing there was a birthday party to look forward to.

The next Sunday, the nurses helped us into wheelchairs for the party—all except Shirley, who couldn't sit up that long. I thought twelve o'clock would never come.

Mother and Dad brought balloons and party hats. Art came, and his presence excited all of us even more. Dad took movies of the festivities. Dorothy blushed and looked away from the camera while Renée mugged shamelessly. Shirley self-consciously waved whenever the camera was pointed at her, and Alice put her hands over her face and refused to be photographed.

Mother opened a large box, revealing a chocolate birthday cake with thirteen candles. The nurses were invited to share the cake, so there was quite a group crowded into the room to sing "Happy Birthday." As I blew out the candles, I had only one wish: *I want to walk again.*

After we ate cake, I opened my presents. Dorothy and

Renée had made a bead bracelet for me in their occupational therapy class. Alice had made a card, which surprised me, because on the morning of the party, she pretended to have forgotten all about my birthday. Shirley was not well enough to make anything, but her name had been added to Alice's card.

We hated to have the afternoon end, but as usual, my parents gave us something to look forward to.

"Next week," Dad said, "you can see yourselves in the movie."

"Not me," said Alice. "I'm not in it."

"Yes, you are," said Dad. "I got some shots of you when you didn't know it."

Alice grumbled about that, but when Sunday rolled around again, she was eager to see the film.

There was much bustling about as my parents set up the projector and screen and hung bedspreads over the windows to darken the room. Dorothy and Renée were in their wheelchairs and so was I, but Shirley's bed had to be pushed across the room next to Alice's so that everyone could see.

Dorothy had never seen herself in a movie, and she shouted with excitement each time she appeared on screen. Alice kept saying, "There we are! That's us!"

When the movie ended, we begged Dad to rewind it and play it again, which he did.

In bed that night, the other girls talked about how much fun it was to see themselves in a movie. Listening to their chatter, I remembered dozens of other home movies—of me playing with B.J., riding my bike, and climbing a tree. There was footage of me modeling a new coat and riding my friend's pony.

As I compared those other, happy times to my hospital birthday party, I felt homesick. It had been a wonderful party, and I was grateful for it, but it wasn't as good as being well.

Will it ever happen? I wondered. Will I ever ride a bike again?

My worries were eased by Miss Ballard's optimistic outlook. She praised my progress every day, saying things like, "If you keep this up, you'll be walking soon." After she had worked with me for a week, Miss Ballard asked if I would like to try a hot bath instead of the hot packs.

"Anything would be better than hot packs," I said.

The next morning two of the nurses, Willie and Terry, helped me into a large bathtub that was partly filled with

SMALL STEPS: THE YEAR I GOT POLIO

hot water. Then Willie turned the hot water on again. "We'll let it run until the water is as hot as you can take it," she said.

The water got hotter and hotter, but because it happened gradually, I didn't mind. When the tub was full, I soaked until the water cooled down, emerging with lobster-red skin and fingers and toes as wrinkled as raisins.

I dressed and had my physical therapy session. "Do you want to have a bath each day instead of hot packs?" Miss Ballard asked.

I grinned. "No more hot packs? Ever?"

"No more hot packs." She made a note on my chart.

I loved the hot baths. They relaxed and soothed my muscles even more than the hot packs had, without the initial burning sensation. Also, my arms and legs felt weightless in the water; I could move them in ways that I could not otherwise.

A daily trip to the occupational therapy room was added to my schedule. O.T. consisted of crafts and projects designed to strengthen damaged muscles.

On my way to the O.T. room, I went through a ward for younger children. Several were playing with dolls. The dolls all lay on their backs while the children moved the dolls' arms and legs around. One little girl told her doll, "This will hurt, but it will help you get well." I wondered if there were doll-size hot packs.

When I reached O.T., I saw other patients painting, weaving scarves, and making belts. I was eager to start my own craft project.

The occupational therapist, whose name was Jeanette, took the footrest off my wheelchair. "We'll need your shoes and socks off, too," she said, and quickly removed them. I could not imagine what craft project required me to have bare feet.

Jeanette dumped a bag of marbles in a pile next to my right foot. "Pick them up with your toes," she said, "one at a time, and move them over to your other foot."

I stared at her. "Why?"

"It's good exercise for your feet and ankles."

I curled my right toes around a green marble, moved my foot to the left, and released the marble.

"Very good!" Jeanette said.

"This," I muttered, "is the stupidest thing I've ever done."

"It won't take long," Jeanette said. "There are only seventy-five marbles."

"I'll die of boredom," I complained, but Jeanette had already gone on to show some lucky patient how to make a belt.

When half the marbles had been moved, I told Jeanette, "My leg is tired. I can't do any more."

"Use your other foot," she replied. "Move the marbles back where they were to start with."

Later in the week, I made a coin purse in O.T. In the hospital, I had no use for a coin purse, but it was better than picking up marbles with my toes.

11: Dancing the Hula, Popping a Wheelie

Just before Thanksgiving, Miss Ballard announced, "Tomorrow you're going to stand by yourself."

I knew my physical therapy sessions were helping me. My arms and legs were stronger. My back was stronger, too; I could now sit up for several hours at a time. Still, I worried all evening. I remembered trying to stand alone at University Hospital.

The next morning, Miss Ballard helped me sit with my feet over the side of the bed. She put one arm around my waist and said, "Slide off until your feet hit the floor. Then lock your knees."

"Isn't someone going to help us?" I asked. "What if I fall?"

"I won't let you fall," she said. I didn't see how she could stop me if I collapsed, since I was bigger than she was. Probably, we would both go down.

Alice, whose bed was closest to mine, stared at me but

said nothing. I wondered if she hoped I would fall. It had to be hard for her to watch new patients arrive, get better, and leave while she always remained behind with her condition unchanged.

A soft voice from across the room said, "Good luck." Dorothy, who might never stand alone, crossed her fingers.

My fear vanished. I slid forward and put my feet on the floor. With Miss Ballard's hand firmly on my waist, I locked my knees, and stood.

When Miss Ballard let go, I remained standing. I stood straight and steady, with no support, for a full minute, beaming at Dorothy the whole time.

"That's fine," said Miss Ballard.

"Good show," said Dorothy.

"From now on," said Miss Ballard, as she helped me sit on the bed, "you'll stand for awhile every day. Soon you'll be able to get in and out of the wheelchair by yourself."

Each day I stood alone a little longer, and my confidence grew like Jack's beanstalk. Unfortunately, it grew a bit faster than my strength and soon got me into trouble.

One evening, we were all in our beds, talking about

trips we wanted to take. I said I would like to go to Hawaii and learn to do the hula.

"What's the hula?" Alice asked.

I explained that it's a traditional Hawaiian dance where the dancers wear grass skirts and sway their hips in time to the music.

"I never heard of any hula," Alice said. "Are you making this up?"

"I'll show you," I said. I flung back the blankets, swung my legs over the side of the bed, and stood up.

I put both hands off to one side and tried to sway my hips back and forth. Instantly, I crashed to the floor, landing in a heap by the side of my bed. I was strong enough to stand alone briefly, but I was clearly not ready to dance the hula.

When the other girls saw me go down, they panicked.

"Nurse!" screamed Shirley.

"Peg fell!" shouted Dorothy.

Alice punched her call button over and over, which made a red light and a buzzer go on at the nurses' station.

"Help! Help!" everyone yelled together.

Willie was close by, and she broke all speed records dashing to our room. When she saw me lying on the floor, she knelt beside me. "Are you hurt?" she asked. "Why were you out of bed?"

I looked up at her. "I was doing the hula," I said.

"The *hula?*"

"Alice didn't know what the hula is," explained Renée.

"So Peg was going to show her," Dorothy added.

Shaking her head in disbelief, Willie helped me into bed and warned me to stay there. "In all my years of nursing," she said, "I've never had a polio patient try to dance the hula."

Although I wasn't hurt, I was a bit shaken, and I meekly promised not to do the hula again.

"Good," said Willie. "What would I write in my report? 'Patient broke leg doing the hula'?" She began to laugh, and soon all of us had a runaway case of the giggles.

For days afterward, patients and staff asked me, "Is it true that you tried to do the hula?" When I admitted that I had, the response was always the same: incredulous laughter.

My strength increased daily, and I was measured for a pair of walking sticks. If I could learn to walk with sticks, I wouldn't need the wheelchair any longer.

Walking sticks are similar to crutches except shorter. Instead of going under the armpits, they end just below the elbow. A ring of metal circles the patient's arm at the top of each stick, and there is a wooden crossbar to hold on to.

"Why do I have to wait for new sticks to get here?" I asked. "Dorothy already has a pair, and she only uses them an hour a day. She won't care if I borrow them."

"It is important," Miss Ballard said, "for the walking sticks to be exactly the right height for you. If they are too short, even by only an inch, you would have to lean forward, which would cause back problems. If the sticks are too long, you would not be able to use all of your arm strength for balance."

Willie told me that using sticks strengthened the leg muscles. "If you can walk with sticks," she said, "you may get so strong you won't need them anymore."

I asked Miss Ballard if this was true.

"No two cases are the same," she said. Then she smiled and added, "I hope you'll learn to walk with them and then to walk without them."

Every morning I greeted Miss Ballard with, "Are my sticks here yet?" Each day I was told to be patient.

"They are made in Canada," she said, "and each pair is cut to be exactly the right size. It takes time."

"Too much time," I complained. While I waited, I learned to get from my bed to the wheelchair by myself. This new skill was a giant step on the road to independence. Now I could get out of bed any time I wanted. I could go to the O.T. room or visit someone in a different ward or simply wheel myself up and down the halls.

I liked to talk with other people, and I spent a lot of time visiting patients who didn't get any outside company. Remembering how Tommy had enjoyed hearing my books, I began reading aloud to the little kids every day. I chatted with some of the adult patients, too, especially one who told about all the pets she had at home. I loved hearing about her animals, even though it made me lonesome for B.J.

The bad news, as far as the staff was concerned, was that I soon became a daredevil in my wheelchair. My favorite trick was to "pop a wheelie." I pushed my wheelchair as fast as I could. When I got to top speed, I yanked on both hand brakes. This forced the large back wheels of the chair to stop so suddenly that the two small front wheels raised off the floor. I leaned against the seat as I sat tilted back with my feet in the air.

I received several warnings about what would happen to me if I tipped up too high and crashed over backward, but I did my stunt whenever the nurses weren't looking.

I never showed my parents this trick because I knew they would forbid me to do it. My roommates never mentioned it to them, either, even though the other girls frequently requested a demonstration when we were alone. I was always happy to tear down the hall and pop a wheelie at the doorway of our room.

My new mobility made it easier to get the food my parents brought, which was stashed under my bed. (The beds were high.) Friends and neighbors of my family, hearing about the four girls who didn't get much company, loaded my parents with home-baked brownies, animal crackers, and tins of peanuts. Mother added bags of apples and oranges and bunches of bananas. It was a regular supermarket under my bed.

During my first weeks at the Sheltering Arms, the only way we could have a snack was to ask a nurse to get it for us. Often we were told it was too close to mealtime, or the nurse was busy right then, or we had already eaten too many treats that day.

After I learned to get out of bed alone, I would sit in my wheelchair and grasp the arm with my left hand so I wouldn't fall out while I reached under my bed. My wooden back scratcher, a gift from Grandpa, hooked cookie containers and pulled them out from under the bed far more often than it scratched my back.

Since a fresh load of food arrived each Sunday, we felt compelled to eat everything before Saturday night. I piled the goodies in my lap and wheeled from bed to bed distributing them, not caring how close it was to mealtime or how many cookies we had already eaten that day.

As we munched cookies after dinner one Wednesday, Willie came in and said, "Peg, you have a visitor in the lobby."

"Me?" I said.

"I don't see anyone else named Peg," remarked Alice.

"Who is it?" I asked.

Willie shrugged. "He didn't give his name."

"*He?*" said Renée, and Willie nodded mysteriously.

"It must be Art," I said.

"If it was Art," Renée said, "he would have asked for Dorothy."

"Art would come up to our room," said Shirley.

"Is he tall, dark, and handsome?" Renée asked.

"No," said Willie. "He's tall, blonde, and cute."

"Whoo, whoo," said Renée. "You didn't tell us you have a boyfriend!"

Quickly I combed my hair and got into my wheelchair. I couldn't imagine who my visitor was. I wheeled into the elevator, rode to the first floor, and went out to the lobby.

"Hello, Peg."

"Dr. Bevis!" He was even better-looking in street clothes than in his white uniform. I was overjoyed to see him.

"I came to see how my favorite patient is doing," he said. "Believe it or not, I miss your knock, knock jokes."

I told him about my roommates and about the hot baths and about my physical therapy treatments with Miss Ballard.

"I've talked with her on the telephone several times," he said. "She tells me you are an exemplary patient and very brave."

I wasn't sure what *exemplary* meant, but from the way he said it, I figured it was a compliment. I hoped he would report the part about being brave to Mrs. Crab.

"How is Tommy?" I asked.

"When I left, he was listening to the 'Lone Ranger,'" Dr. Bevis said.

"Is he still in the iron lung?"

"Yes. For now."

Dr. Bevis didn't stay long, but his visit left me glowing with pleasure. His parting words were, "Don't forget. You're going to come back to University Hospital and walk for me."

"I'll be there," I said, and this time we both knew it was more than wishful thinking. I just might make it.

12: A Disappointing Trip

"Lights out!"

Each night at nine the call rang out, and a nurse flicked the switch, darkening our room. We rarely protested. Sometimes we talked for awhile in the dark, but most nights we were ready to go to sleep. Breakfast arrived early, and the struggle to do ordinary activities was tiring.

On the night of my visit from Dr. Bevis, however, we talked for a long time, sharing memories of doctors and nurses and treatments.

These memories led to talk about when we got polio and how we first learned what was wrong with us.

Dorothy said, "I was sick for three days before my parents could get me into town to a doctor. By then, my legs were paralyzed, and I had trouble breathing. When I got to the hospital, I went in the iron lung right away, and they couldn't start the hot packs and muscle stretching until I came out." There was no hint of regret about this delay; sweet Dorothy simply stated the facts and accepted them.

Renée and Shirley told similar stories of not getting medical help until after they were paralyzed, and of time in an iron lung delaying the Kenny treatments.

"It didn't matter when they brought me to the hospital," Alice said. "The Kenny treatments weren't used when I got polio."

"You never had hot packs?" I asked. "Or physical therapy?"

"Nope."

My first reaction was, lucky you, no Torture Time. But I instantly realized it wasn't lucky at all. Alice might not have had "dropfoot" if she had received hot packs and stretching. She might have been able to stand or even walk.

I wondered what my condition would be if I had not received the Sister Kenny treatments. Would my hands be deformed from permanently tight muscles, like those of some patients I had seen? Would my legs be withered from disuse? Would I, like Shirley, be unable to sit up more than an hour at a time?

We also talked about our homes and families, and about what we missed the most.

Shirley said, "I miss my grandma. When I was little, she used to sing me to sleep."

Alice said, "I'll sing you to sleep," and she began to sing, "Rock-a-bye, baby, on the tree top."

This was the first time I had heard Alice sing; she had a clear, strong soprano voice. After listening to Alice's song, nobody said another word. We didn't want to break the mood of her lullaby.

The next night after lights out, I said, "Alice, I know how to harmonize. If you'll sing soprano on some songs, I'll sing alto."

Alice sang: "Shine on, shine on harvest moon, up in the sky."

I chimed in with the harmony. "I ain't had no lovin' since January, February, June or July."

Dorothy giggled at the lyrics. Alice and I sang on.

My mother's family used to go on picnics, and as dusk fell, all the aunts, uncles, and cousins would sit around the campfire, singing. Mother always sang as she worked around the house, too, and when I was small, she often sang songs to entertain me. Whenever my family traveled, we sang in the car as a way to pass the time. Because music had always been part of my life, I knew all the words to many songs.

Alice, whose main source of entertainment for years was listening to the radio, knew many songs, too. Dorothy and Renée also loved to sing. Because Shirley's breathing was shallow, the rest of us couldn't hear her sing, but she said she liked to try.

From then on, every night after lights out, we all sang in the dark. We sang "Blue Skies" and "I've Been Workin' on the Railroad" and "You Are My Sunshine." We sang rounds: "Row, Row, Row Your Boat" and "Three Blind Mice."

One night we sang longer than usual, doing all of our favorite songs and thinking of new ones that we hadn't done before. After more than an hour of this, Dorothy remarked, "I'm hungry."

"So am I," said Renée.

"Hold everything," I said. "Food is on the way."

"You can't turn on the light," Alice said. "The nurses will see it."

"I won't turn on the light."

"You're going to get up in the dark?" squeaked Shirley.

"I don't need to see. I can feel the wheelchair, and I know where the food is."

I got in my wheelchair, fished out a box of cookies, and made the rounds of the other beds in the dark. I felt daring and heroic, and only slightly guilty.

"Thanks," whispered Renée.

"You saved my life," whispered Dorothy. "I was starving."

"Me, too," said Alice.

Shirley said nothing, but she took two cookies and ate them.

I parked Silver, climbed back in bed, and was munching on peanut-butter cookies when the door opened and a nurse peeked in. There wasn't a sound in Room 202. Not even any chewing.

December shivered in, and Miss Ballard told me that my parents had asked permission to take me home for an overnight visit.

"Do I get to go?" I asked.

"It isn't usually done," she told me, "but you are getting along well, and your parents want to try it. If you want to go, I will give permission."

"Of course I want to go," I said. "Why wouldn't I?"

"It will be hard to get around at home," she said.

"I don't care. When do I leave?"

The arrangements were made for the following weekend. I was to be picked up at noon on Saturday and returned Sunday evening.

Even though Miss Ballard didn't usually work on Saturday, she was there when my parents arrived. She had written detailed instructions about what I could and could not do.

"Be careful getting her into the wheelchair," she warned. "Be sure the brakes are locked, or it will scoot away from her. Don't let her get too tired. She should not have any visitors besides your immediate family, and she needs to go to bed by nine o'clock, and—"

"Miss Ballard," Mother interrupted. "She is our daughter. We'll take good care of her; I promise."

Miss Ballard nodded and kept quiet, but she looked nervous as I was helped from the wheelchair into the back seat of our green Oldsmobile.

Sunlight glinted on the snow, and the fresh air smelled wonderful. The other girls had told me that in warm weather they were wheeled around the grounds, but since I arrived it had been too cold to go outside.

It was a two-hour ride. Seat belts were not yet used in passenger cars, so there was nothing to help me stay upright.

I had never realized how much I depended on my leg and back muscles to keep my balance in the car. The motion made me tilt from side to side, and I was unable to steady myself. When we went around a curve, I had to grasp the armrest and hang on to prevent myself from falling over sideways.

My parents were not aware of my problem, and I didn't tell them. I wanted to be well enough to go home for good, and if I admitted how weak I was, we would all know that I wasn't well enough. By the time we got home, I was so tired from the effort of trying to stay upright that I could barely make it into my wheelchair.

Our house had two front steps. As I pushed my wheelchair up the sidewalk to the front door, the steps loomed in front of me like Mt. McKinley. How was I going to get in the house?

Dad realized my predicament. He grabbed the handles of my chair and turned it around so I faced the street. Then, with great effort, he pulled me up the steps. I couldn't brace my feet against the footrest because I had so little strength in my legs. I gripped the arms of the wheelchair and hoped he wouldn't dump me.

Silver balked when it was time to cross the threshold. Dad yanked mightily. The sudden jolt pitched me forward; I clutched the chair to keep from tumbling face-first down the steps.

It was great to see Grandpa, although when he saw the wheelchair, he looked so unhappy that I felt I should apologize.

B.J. didn't care whether I could walk or not. He barked and ran in circles and slurped my hands.

Mother had prepared all of my favorite foods: macaroni and cheese, green beans, Waldorf salad, and for dessert, cream puffs. Mother's cream puffs were six inches across, filled with whipped cream, and topped with homemade hot fudge sauce. I always requested them for birthdays and special company.

I was unable to push my wheelchair on the carpeting; Dad had to push me into the dining room. The arms of my wheelchair were too high to fit under the table, so I had to be helped into a regular chair. Once there, I couldn't slide the chair forward. By the time I was in place, I was too discouraged to eat much.

The first floor of our house had a tiny half-bath consisting of a toilet and sink. My wheelchair did not fit in it. To get the chair close enough to the toilet, I had to leave the door open. There was no bar on the wall to hold onto, like there was at the Sheltering Arms, so I needed help to get off the toilet. The lack of privacy embarrassed me.

Since going upstairs was out of the question, I slept on a cot in the living room.

I had longed to come home but now that I was there, it wasn't much fun. Home wasn't the same if I couldn't sleep in my own bedroom or use the bathroom by myself. It wasn't the same when I couldn't sit down at the table without help. I felt like a stranger in those familiar rooms. When it was time to go to sleep, I wished I had someone to sing with.

In the morning, I practiced one of my piano lessons and discovered that my foot could no longer work the sustain pedal. When B.J. brought his rag toy to me, I wasn't strong enough to play tug, as I used to. My friend Karen called, but when the phone rang, I couldn't move my chair across the carpet to answer it. I had to wait for Grandpa to push me.

At noon, it began to snow. Dad and Mother decided

we should leave early in case the roads were icy. I did not object; I was ready to return to the hospital. Trying to get along in the normal world was too hard. I still needed more help than my well-meaning family could provide.

The ride was even more tiring this time because I was weary at the start from the effort and excitement of my time at home. Once again, I clung to the armrest and struggled to keep my balance in the back seat.

Because of the snow, it took longer than usual to get back to Minneapolis. I grew more uncomfortable every minute. With relief and gladness, I returned to the welcoming embrace of the Sheltering Arms.

Miss Ballard questioned me at length on Monday morning. When I confessed that I had been glad to come back, she smiled ruefully and said, "I was afraid of that. But I had to let you try."

"Silver almost threw me," I said, "going up the steps to my house."

Miss Ballard looked horrified and covered her ears with her hands. "I don't want to hear about it," she said.

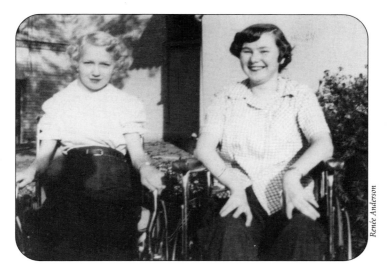

My hospital roommates, Shirley (left) and Dorothy.

Some of the intern staff at University of Minnesota Hospital in Minneapolis, spring 1950. Dr. Bevis is third from the right in the second row.

Alice (left) and Dorothy.

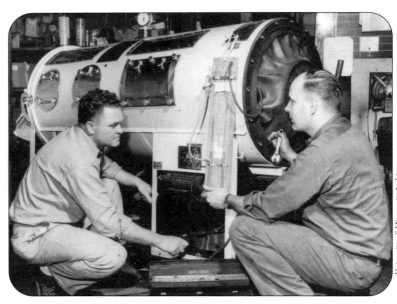

An iron lung at the University of Minnesota Hospital.

Renée (left), Dorothy (center), and me: Christmas at Sheltering Arms, 1949.

Miss Ballard helping an unidentified patient.

Art Schulze, my
brother, 1948.

Elizabeth Schulze

My parents, Beth and
Bob Schulze, in 1949.

Elizabeth Schulze

In the summer of 1916, the first major U.S. polio epidemic occurred. New York City was hardest hit. When families with children fled the city, some nearby communities tried to keep them out, fearing children would spread the infection.

One of the rare photographs of President Franklin D. Roosevelt in his wheelchair. Roosevelt was stricken with polio in 1921, before he became president. In this photo taken at Hilltop Cottage, the home in Hyde Park, New York, he built for his retirement, the president holds his dog Fala on his lap and is speaking to Ruthie Bie, the daughter of the cottage's caretakers.

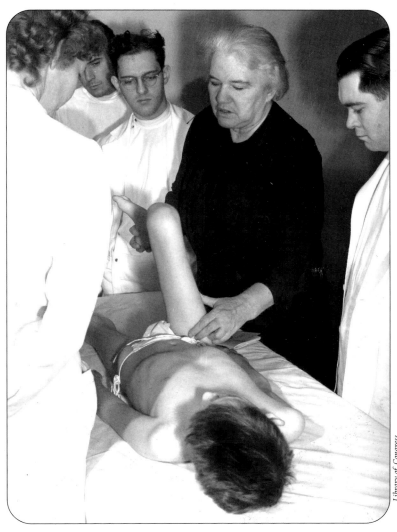

Sister Elizabeth Kenny, an Australian nurse, successfully treated polio patients with hot packs, muscle massage, and stretching exercises. The technique she developed helped me recover. Here she demonstrates her method on a young American polio patient.

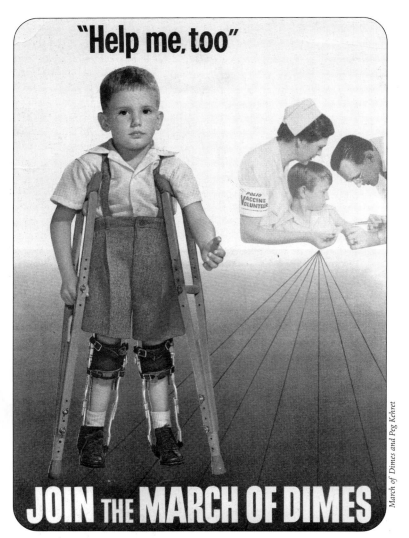

Pictures of appealing children on March of Dimes posters encouraged the public to donate money for research to fight polio. The March of Dimes is an organization whose initial goal was to eliminate polio.

Dr. Jonas Salk and research assistant Ethel Bailey in his laboratory at the University of Pittsburgh, where he developed his killed-virus polio vaccine. The research was funded by the March of Dimes.

In antiques shops, I found some old March of Dimes buttons.
March of Dimes and Peg Kehret

March of Dimes

In 1954, 1.8 million young schoolchildren took part in nationwide trials testing the Salk vaccine. The trials were led by Dr. Thomas Francis, Jr., of the University of Michigan. The vaccine proved successful, and the children were called "Polio Pioneers." They each received the tin button shown above.

March of Dimes and Peg Kehret

On April 12, 1955, the Salk vaccine was pronounced safe and effective. The next morning, newspapers announced the thrilling news; polio would be conquered!

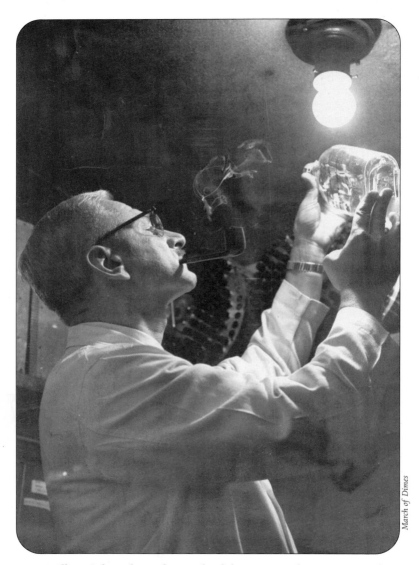

Dr. Albert Sabin, shown here in his laboratory at the University of Cincinnati, developed a live-virus vaccine that was approved for use in the U.S. in 1962. It soon replaced the Salk vaccine. Dr. Sabin's research was also funded by the March of Dimes.

Renée, me, and Dorothy at our reunion in September 1997.

This photo of my husband, Carl, my mother, and me was taken in 1996, the year Small Steps was published. When I first recovered from polio, Mother destroyed every photo of me in the wheelchair or using my walking sticks. She said she didn't want to remember that part of my life. By the time Small Steps was published, she was eager to talk about polio and enjoyed giving copies to her friends.

Peg Kehret

Carl and me with our dog Daisy in front of our motor home in 1997. Pete and Molly, our cats, were inside. After I began writing books for children, we traveled this way for many years when I gave talks at schools, libraries, and conferences.

Peg Kehret

I'm wearing my "award necklace," which has a charm for every state where I've won the Young Reader Award for my children's books. Each charm is engraved on the back with an abbreviation of the winning book's title and the year that it won. The photo is from 2001. There are presently twenty-five charms on the necklace.

Peg Kehret

Peg Kehret

In 1957, the U.S. Postal Service issued a three-cent stamp honoring those who helped fight polio. A thirty-three-cent stamp titled "Polio Vaccine Developed" was issued as part of a 1999 sheet of commemorative stamps. For both stamps, special "first day of issue" envelopes were created for collectors. Dr. Salk and Dr. Sabin were both honored with new stamps in 2006.

13: The Great
Accordion Concert

Although I had not yet mastered the fine art of moving the pile of marbles from spot to spot with my toes, I received a new challenge in O.T. I was going to learn to play the accordion.

Certain muscles of the arms and hands are used when pushing an accordion in and out, and it happened that I needed help with those particular muscles. The Sheltering Arms owned an accordion, and Miss Ballard knew I'd had two years of piano lessons. She said the accordion was the perfect exercise for me.

From my very first attempt, I hated the accordion. It was heavy and awkward, and pushing it in and out made my arms ache. The trick of playing a melody on the keyboard with one hand, pushing the proper chord buttons with the other hand, and at the same time pushing and pulling on the accordion itself was completely beyond me.

"It would be easier if you asked me to juggle and tap dance at the same time," I said.

"You just need practice," Miss Ballard replied. "Try a little longer."

I did try. However, even when I got the correct right-hand note with the proper left-hand chord and pushed air through the bellows at the same time, I didn't care for the sound. I had never liked accordion music, and my efforts during O.T. did nothing to change my mind.

When my parents heard about the accordion, Mother said, "What fun! You've always loved your piano lessons."

"That's different," I said. "I like the way a piano sounds."

"You already know how to read music," Dad pointed out. "You will master that accordion in no time."

I insisted I would never be adept on the accordion, and Dad kept saying it would be a breeze.

I finally said, "Why don't *you* play it, if you think it's so easy?"

"All right. I will," said Dad, and off he went to the O.T. room to borrow the accordion.

He came back with the shoulder straps in place and an eager look on his face. My dad played piano by ear, so he didn't need sheet music. Even so, the sounds he produced could only be called squawks and squeaks.

He pushed and pulled. He punched the buttons. He grew red in the face. Beads of perspiration popped out on his bald spot. Something vaguely resembling the first few notes of "Beer Barrel Polka" emerged from the accordion, but they were accompanied by assorted other sounds, none of which could be called musical.

We girls covered our ears, made faces, and booed. We pointed our thumbs down. Mother laughed until tears ran down her cheeks.

Finally, Dad admitted defeat. Temporary defeat.

"I'll try again next week," he said. "Meanwhile, I want you to keep practicing."

"It will sound just as terrible next week," I said, but I agreed to work on my accordion technique awhile longer.

The following Sunday, we could hardly wait to tease Dad about his musical fiasco.

"When do we get the accordion concert?" Renée asked the minute my parents arrived.

"Wait!" exclaimed Alice. "I want to put in my earplugs."

We teased until Dad reluctantly agreed to try it again.

We snickered and tee-heed as he brought the O.T. accordion into the room. He sat on a chair and carefully adjusted the straps.

"Quit stalling," I said.

"What's the rush?" said Renée as she put her fingers in her ears.

Dad began to play. Instead of squeaks and squawks, he played "Beer Barrel Polka" flawlessly, from start to finish.

Our jaws dropped. We gazed at him and at each other in astonishment. When he finished the song, our questions exploded like a string of firecrackers. "How did you learn to play?" "Who taught you?" "Where did you get an accordion?" He simply smiled, while Mother applauded.

Then they told us the whole story. He had rented an accordion from a music store and practiced every spare second in order to surprise us with his concert.

"Can you play any other songs?" I asked.

"It took me all week to learn that one," Dad said.

"And he stayed up until midnight every night, practicing," Mother added.

After that, I didn't dare complain about my accordion sessions. I never did get as good at it as Dad got in just seven days, but I managed to produce a few recognizable tunes, and the effort did help strengthen my arm muscles and my fingers.

The Sheltering Arms had a school which Dorothy, Renée, Alice, and I attended. Shirley was supposed to go, too, but because of her weak back, she could only sit up in a wheelchair for an hour at a time, so she didn't always make it to class.

The staff consisted of one dedicated, overworked teacher, Mrs. West, who tried to help dozens of children of varying ages and educational backgrounds. It should have been an impossible task, made even harder by the fact that all of the students had physical disabilities, yet the school was orderly and effective.

Students in wheelchairs got a wooden desktop which attached to the arms of the wheelchair and provided a writing surface. I loved my new desk; for the first time since I got polio, it was comfortable to write. The desktop also made it easier and less tiring to hold a book.

The school had a small library, and Mrs. West recommended books to us. A librarian from the Minneapolis Public Library brought books once a week and was always willing to take requests. I stopped reading books for children and began reading adult books. I read *The Hunchback of Notre Dame* and *War and Peace* and *The Scarlet Letter*.

Because hot baths, physical therapy, and O.T. took up much of my time, I was in school for only two hours a day. I hungered for more. I especially liked hearing books read aloud and writing book reports.

Mrs. West had several seventh-grade textbooks, but they were not the same books that I had in my school at home. She suggested that I try to get the same books that my classmates in Austin were using. "That way, you won't be so far behind when you go home," she said.

My mother talked to the principal in Austin, who agreed that Mother should bring me textbooks from each of my classes, along with the weekly assignments that the other kids were doing. Because I had already missed so many weeks of classes and my hand still tired quickly when I wrote, I was not required to write the assignments or turn in any homework.

At the end of the school year, I would take the same final exams that the other kids in my grade took for each class. If I passed, I would go on to eighth grade. If I failed, I would be held back a year to repeat those classes.

No one ever told me to read my history assignments or study my math. It was up to me. Since I did not intend to be a grade behind my friends, I gladly taught myself.

Alice was interested in my schoolwork, especially my history lessons. Whenever I told her what I was reading, she listened carefully. Sometimes she asked questions which forced me to go back to my book for the answers. Other times, we had lively discussions which we both enjoyed. I learned to respect Alice's intellect, and I kidded her about getting a job as my tutor.

The school had a collection of newspaper and magazine articles about Sister Kenny. Curious about the woman who invented Torture Time, I read them. I had assumed Sister Kenny was a Catholic nun. She was not. "Sister" is an Australian military term, the equivalent of a first lieutenant in the United States Army. Elizabeth Kenny was commissioned "sister" while serving as a nurse in World War I.

Sister Kenny developed her unique treatments accidentally. While on vacation in the bush country of Australia in 1903, she was asked to help a sick child. Polio was not yet a common disease, and she had no idea what was wrong with the little girl, who was in extreme pain and unable to straighten one arm and one leg. There was no telephone, and no doctor or hospital nearby.

Sister Kenny had a special interest in and knowledge of muscles because her younger brother's muscles had been weak when he was a child. She had developed exercises for him even before she began her nurse's training. She recognized that the little girl's agony was caused by severe muscle spasms, and she knew the relaxing power of heat. She tore a wool blanket into strips, dipped them in boiling water, wrung them out, and placed them on the child. The little girl stopped crying and fell asleep.

Each time the little girl awoke in pain, Sister Kenny applied more hot packs. As the muscles relaxed, she gently massaged the child's arm and leg until the girl was able to straighten them.

A second child soon showed the same symptoms, and once again Sister Kenny eased the pain with hot packs and massage. Using her knowledge of muscles, she suggested exercises for the children to do as soon as they were well enough.

When she was finally able to discuss these cases with a doctor, she learned that her patients had suffered from infantile paralysis (the original name for polio), and that her treatment had never before been tried. The doctor was amazed to learn that both children had recovered.

Family friends heard of her success in the bush country and asked her to treat their child. As polio epidemics increased, so did reports of Sister Kenny's unorthodox treatments, and other people sought her help for their children. Not all patients recovered completely, but many did, especially those who received treatment early in their illness.

The Australian doctors ignored her successes and didn't try her ideas. She opened her own small clinic, and her methods worked so well that she began training other people to use them so she could open additional clinics.

The Australian medical officials, however, refused to sanction her work. In 1938, at the height of a polio epidemic, they issued a lengthy report to the public which stated that Sister Kenny's methods were mistaken and unnecessary.

Discouraged by this rejection, Sister Kenny left her homeland in 1940 and traveled to the United States, settling in Minnesota. Word of her unusual methods preceded her, and when she arrived in the U.S., she was greeted by newspaper reporters. Possibly because the newspapers created high public interest, doctors in the United States gave her a chance to demonstrate her methods.

They were astounded by her results. Badly crippled patients showed rapid improvement if they began the Kenny treatments soon enough.

News of her accomplishments spread, and many doctors in Minneapolis asked Sister Kenny to work with their polio patients. Soon her procedures were widely accepted, and in December 1942, the Sister Kenny Institute, a facility for teaching her theories and methods, was dedicated in Minneapolis. Eventually, her methods were adopted all over the world, including Australia.

As I read, I realized how fortunate I was that by the time I was stricken with polio, the Kenny method was the standard treatment for cases like mine. Previously, many polio patients were put in splints and casts to keep their arms and legs straight.

Polio causes muscle spasms which feel much like the familiar "charley-horse" cramp that people sometimes get in their legs. The spasms caused people's arms and legs to bend, and without treatment the limbs sometimes stayed bent permanently. The casts were intended to prevent that.

I remembered the severe cramps that bent my knees when I first got polio and imagined how it would have felt if my legs had been put into casts. By comparison, Torture Time seemed like a picnic.

Prior to Sister Kenny, some patients were left in casts for years. When the casts were finally removed, the patients could not move their limbs at all because muscles which are never used waste away. Because of the casts, even muscles not affected by polio became withered.

I didn't need to read statistics to know that the Kenny method worked; all I had to do was move my arms and legs. I was getting better, and hers was the only treatment I had received. If I had gotten sick a few years earlier, while Sister Kenny was still in Australia, my future would surely have been dreary.

14: Good-bye, Silver;
Hello, Sticks

My walking sticks finally came. As I rubbed my fingers across the smooth wood, I felt as excited as I had when I got my bicycle. I could hardly wait to try them.

"Go slowly," Miss Ballard cautioned after she showed me how to hold the sticks. "Take small steps. Slow and easy."

I listened impatiently, eager to get on with the business of walking. At last the sticks were in my hands, and I was on my feet. Miss Ballard stood beside me, ready to help if I needed her. I was confident that I could stride forward on my own. I was Supergirl, ready to conquer the world.

"On your mark," I said.

"Go slowly," Miss Ballard repeated.

"Get set..."

"Easy," said Miss Ballard. "Slow and easy."

"Go!"

I lurched forward, unsteady and awkward.

"Small steps!" cried Miss Ballard. "Don't try to run."

I wobbled and swayed, barely able to keep my balance. It was not going to be as simple as I had thought.

"It's like learning to walk all over again," Miss Ballard said. "You'll be shaky at first, the way a year-old baby is, but you will do better with practice."

I took her advice about moving slowly—not because I wanted to, but because I wasn't able to move fast. I had to think about the sequence of each step: lift right stick and right foot, move them forward, put them down. Lean on stick for balance. Lift the left stick and the left foot, move them forward, put them down. Slowly, slowly. Small steps. Concentrate.

I felt as if bricks were glued to the soles of my shoes. Trying to lift and move my feet took every ounce of energy I had, and sweat trickled down the back of my neck.

That first day, I took ten small steps, each one slow and deliberate. It was hard to coordinate my arms and my feet, and since my arms were still weak, it took great effort to move and control the wooden sticks. When Miss Ballard said I had gone far enough for the first day,

Supergirl slumped with relief back into her wheelchair.

"Good job," said Miss Ballard.

In spite of my weariness, exhilaration filled me, and I felt compelled to pop a wheelie twice as I raced proudly back to my room.

Each day from then on, I went a little farther and a little farther. One small step at a time.

The other girls watched my rapid progress with enthusiasm. There was never any hint of envy over the fact that I, who had arrived at the Sheltering Arms last, was quickly surpassing the rest of them in physical strength and ability. I suppose it didn't hurt to have parents who treated all of my roommates as extra daughters, but I believe it was more than that. Even homemade peanut-butter cookies do not buy true friendship.

We had the kind of camaraderie that I imagine exists between soldiers who have fought together during a long and difficult war. In our case, the enemy was polio. Our battle medals were wheelchairs, back and leg braces, and walking sticks, and we wore them proudly. We were survivors; whatever handicaps we might be left with, polio had not claimed our lives or our spirits.

Our common experiences of pain and paralysis,

separation from our loved ones, and an unending struggle to regain the full use of our bodies made us members of an elite sorority that outsiders could never join. The success of one member became the success of all, and Shirley, Renée, Dorothy, and Alice cheered when they learned I had taken ten steps all by myself on my new walking sticks. Even if they would never walk with only sticks to aid them, my progress meant a victory for them, too, against our mutual foe.

Two weeks after I got my sticks, Miss Ballard told me I was strong enough to use them exclusively. I didn't need Silver anymore.

"You gave me a lot of good rides," I whispered as I patted Silver's side for the last time. I blinked back tears, feeling foolish. I had looked forward to this day for months, and now that it was here, I was all weepy about leaving my wheelchair behind.

Silver had carried me to school, distributed countless treats, and taken me safely to O.T., my sessions with Miss Ballard, visits with other patients, and special events in the sunroom. I'd had many fine times, including my thirteenth birthday, in that wheelchair. As I thought about them, I realized that even if I had never grown strong enough to leave Silver, I still would have been able to lead a happy life.

I took Silver for a farewell trip, which ended with a high-speed dash down the hall, a screech of brakes, and a final shout of "Hi, yo, Silver! Awa-a-ay!" Teetering on the two rear wheels, I tipped farther back than I had ever gone before. It was a terrific last ride.

15: Plans for a Pageant

In spite of my physical progress, I grew unhappy as Christmas approached. We added holiday songs to our nightly chorus, but somehow, while the other songs made me glad, singing Christmas carols made me lonely.

Many nights, when our music ended, I lay in the dark trying not to cry as I thought of other Decembers. Mother always baked several kinds of Christmas cookies, and I knew I would soon have almond bells, spritz cookies, and Russian teacakes under my bed. But it wouldn't be the same. I wanted to hang around the kitchen, begging for bits of raw dough to eat. I wanted to burst in the door after school, stamping the snow off my boots, and smell spicy gingerbread boys fresh from the oven. I wanted to sit at the kitchen table, surrounded by custard cups filled with colored frostings and tinted sugars, and help Mother decorate the sugar cookie Santas and stars. I wanted to help trim the tree and plunk out "Away in a

Manger" on the piano. I wanted to shake my hoarded allowances out of my piggy bank and shop for gifts to surprise Mother and Dad and Grandpa and Art. I wanted to wrap up a dog treat for B.J. and watch him sniff it and drool on the wrapping paper. In short, I wanted to go home. If I couldn't go home, I wanted to skip Christmas altogether and go straight into January.

One night, as I lay wrapped in homesickness, I heard sniffling from across the room. Dorothy was crying, too.

We were lifted out of our depression by the goodwill and holiday spirit of the community. Carolers came frequently, and there were two wonderful parties, one put on by the Shriners and one by a group called the Aqua Jesters. Both groups provided clowns, music, and treats. For a few hours, we all forgot that we couldn't walk as we laughed at the clowns and applauded the magic tricks and musicians.

Even with all this excitement, I begged to be allowed to go home for Christmas. "Just for two days," I said. "Christmas Eve and Christmas Day."

"You didn't get along so well the first time," Miss Ballard reminded me.

"It will be better this time," I insisted. "If I don't

go home, Santa won't know where to find me."

Miss Ballard rolled her eyes, knowing full well that at age thirteen, I knew all about Santa Claus.

Finally I added the last-ditch, tried-and-true argument of kids everywhere: "All the other kids are going home for Christmas."

She gave me a look that said, No, they aren't, but she agreed to think about it.

While I waited for her decision, I learned that the hospital was going to have a Christmas pageant, with patients playing all of the roles. I was thrilled when Miss Ballard asked me to play the part of Mary, the mother of Jesus.

"You're tall for your age," she said, "and Mary was young."

Before I could get too big-headed about my important role, she added, "And we need someone who can make it from the back of the room to the manger without any help."

"Who is going to be Joseph?" Renée asked.

His name was Kenny, and none of us knew him. He was in the men's ward, and we never ventured there.

"Kenny is being discharged the day after our pageant," Miss Ballard said. "He is almost fully recovered and is strong as an ox. He can even walk by himself."

The hospital's youngest patient, a four-month-old boy, would play the part of Jesus. Patients who did not have roles were enlisted to make programs, angel wings, and halos.

During the next few days, my sessions with Miss Ballard were full of conversation about the pageant. The plan was for an adult patient to read the Christmas story from the Bible while the characters silently enacted their parts, forming a tableau at the front of the O.T. room.

"I'd like to have some music, too," Miss Ballard said.

"Not accordion music," I said.

"I understand there are some good singing voices in Room 202."

I wondered how she knew that, since our singing always took place at night, after she had gone home.

"Maybe all of you could sing a song," she continued.

"Why don't you ask Alice to sing a solo?" I suggested. "She doesn't have a part in the pageant yet."

"Is she good enough?" Miss Ballard asked. "The whole hospital will be there, plus many visitors."

No performer ever had a more enthusiastic agent than Alice had that day as I described her clear, bell-like voice.

That afternoon, Miss Ballard asked Alice to sing a solo in the Christmas pageant.

"Me?" Alice said. "How do you know I can even carry a tune?"

"I've heard reports from someone I trust."

"One of the nurses? Did a nurse tell you I can sing?"

"Could be."

Alice assumed that a nurse had talked to Miss Ballard, and I never let on that it was me. What did it matter who recommended her? The important thing was for her to be part of the pageant.

"What do you want me to sing?"

"One of the familiar Christmas carols would be nice."

"Sing 'Silent Night,'" Renée said. "I get chills every time you sing 'Silent Night.'"

"Yes," agreed Dorothy. "You should sing 'Silent Night.'"

Alice looked over at me. "What do you think?" she asked. "You're the one who's had music lessons."

"'Silent Night' would be perfect."

We had one rehearsal. All I had to do was walk from the back of the O.T. room to the front, with Kenny beside me, and sit on a chair.

"Start walking toward the manger when you hear the word *taxed*," Miss Ballard said. "That's your cue."

Kenny and I nodded.

When all the actors were in place, Miss Ballard said, "Now everyone will stand perfectly still while Alice sings 'Silent Night.' When she's finished, the pageant is over." Since no one had any lines to memorize, we only needed to go through it once, and Alice wasn't asked to sing for the rehearsal.

On the evening of the pageant, dinner was served early. It might have been skipped entirely in our room, since we were far too excited to care about food.

We all warned Alice not to drink her milk. We didn't want phlegm in her throat, spoiling her voice. Dorothy, who was going to be an angel, fretted until the nurse in charge of angels showed up to help her into her wings.

When it was time to leave, Alice panicked. "I can't do it," she said. "Not in front of all those people. What if my voice cracks? What if I forget the words?"

"You won't forget the words to 'Silent Night,'" Dorothy said. "You've sung it to us a hundred times this week."

"When it's time to sing," I told her, "close your

eyes and pretend you're in bed, singing only to us."

"What if I go blank? What if nothing comes out of my mouth?"

"That would be an historic first," Renée said.

"I'm scared," Alice whispered. "I'm afraid I'll goof up."

"If you start to have trouble," I said, "I'll join in and sing with you. Nobody will know it wasn't planned."

"Promise?"

"Promise. But you won't goof up. You have the best singing voice I've ever heard."

The O.T. room was the largest room in the hospital. That night it was crowded with patients, visiting family members, and staff.

A spotlight shone on a crude crèche at one end of the room. Hospital beds, with the heads elevated, ringed the perimeter of the room like bent dominoes. Next were U-shaped rows of wheelchairs, with adults in back and kids in front.

My costume was an ankle-length hospital gown belted with a piece of rope. A long piece of deep blue fabric, worn on my head and draped over one shoulder, made me feel slightly more holy.

Miss Ballard rearranged the material three times before it suited her. "You look exactly the way Mary should look," she declared.

"Except for my feet," I said. "Mary didn't wear saddle shoes."

"You need the support of sturdy shoes. I don't want Mary falling on her face before she gets to the manger."

"I should be barefoot. Couldn't I go barefoot just for that short way?"

"No," Miss Ballard said, and I knew by the way she said it that I would be wasting my breath to ask again.

I waited with the other actors just outside the O.T. room door. I hardly recognized Kenny, who wore a long brown bathrobe, a fake beard, and a scarf pulled tight across his forehead and hanging down the back of his neck. I noticed that he was barefoot.

"I thought you'd have a pillow under your dress," Kenny said. "You're supposed to be pregnant."

That had not occurred to me. I asked Willie for a pillow.

"No pillow," she said. "It could throw you off balance."

Miss Ballard rushed out and said, "There's a problem.

So many people came that they didn't keep the aisle as wide as they were supposed to. There isn't room for Mary and Joseph to go down side by side, as planned." She looked at Kenny. "Joseph," she said, "you'll have to follow behind Mary."

Opinions erupted like popping corn from the rest of the cast.

"Mary and Joseph need to be together."

"We should have decorated a wheelchair to look like a donkey, and Kenny could have pushed her."

"Maybe somebody else should be Mary. Can't anyone around here walk alone?"

Nervous that I was going to be replaced at the last second, I said, "If Kenny helps me, I can make it without my sticks."

The babble of voices ceased, and everyone looked at Miss Ballard.

"Without your sticks, you and Kenny would fit in the aisle at the same time," she said. "If Kenny had his arm around your waist to support you, I think you could do it."

Twice during my physical therapy sessions, I had walked short distances holding onto a metal bar attached to the wall while Miss Ballard stood on my other side with her arm around me for support.

"Do you think you can keep her upright?" Miss Ballard asked Kenny. "Can you catch her if she stumbles?"

"Yes," said Kenny, "as long as we use my good arm."

There was no time to practice. The lights in the O.T. room dimmed, and the reader began. "And it came to pass in those days, that there went out a decree from Caesar Augustus, that all the world should be taxed."

Taxed! I thrust my walking sticks at Miss Ballard. Kenny's arm went firmly around my waist, holding and lifting me so my feet barely touched the floor.

"Are you sure you can make it?" Miss Ballard whispered.

I nodded. I wasn't sure at all, but it was too late to change plans. Every eye in the hospital was watching us.

16: Christmas

"*Right foot first,*" Joseph said softly.

The reader continued. As the familiar words rang out, Joseph and Mary slowly made their way to the manger. My legs were far too weak to support my weight without my sticks, but Kenny's strong grip never loosened, and he practically carried me the whole way. Even so, I was glad I had my shoes on.

Our progress was slower than the reader's voice, so when we were only halfway to the front, he quit reading and waited for us to catch up with the story.

When we got to the crèche, Kenny helped me sit down on the chair on one side of the manger, and he sat on the other side.

The reader continued. "And she gave birth to her first-born son and wrapped him in swaddling clothes and laid him in a manger." A nurse from the pediatrics ward stepped forward and placed the baby in the manger.

The other characters entered on cue. Dorothy looked suitably angelic with gauze wings trailing behind her wheelchair and a halo on her head. The wise men entered last, two in wheelchairs and one in braces, carrying gifts that looked suspiciously like the decorated jewelry boxes we had made in O.T. the week before.

We had been directed to hold still while Alice sang her solo. Every character except one followed instructions. Jesus kicked his feet and waved his fists at us.

Alice's voice rang out confidently from the back of the room. "Silent night, holy night. All is calm, all is bright..." Her rendition was flawless: clear, true notes strung together in a necklace of sound, a gift for everyone in the room to wear.

The last "Sleep in heavenly peace," echoed for several seconds in the silence as visitors, staff, and patients wiped tears from their cheeks. Then thunderous applause broke out. Everyone talked at once, exclaiming how perfect the pageant had been.

Miss Ballard rushed forward with my walking sticks, afraid she had let me do too much.

"Kenny did all the work for me," I said, which was true.

The parents of the baby scooped him from the manger and beamed while others admired him.

But the real star that night was Alice, and she shone brilliantly. Except for her four roommates and whichever nurses had listened outside our door, no one had known until then what a lovely voice she had. She was congratulated and complimented, over and over. People asked if she took voice lessons. She blossomed under all the attention, smiling graciously and talking with anyone who approached her.

Refreshments were served, and our appetites immediately returned. We drank cranberry punch and stuffed ourselves with Christmas cookies, fruitcake, and candy canes.

When the party ended, the five of us went back to our room and celebrated by ourselves. Long after the lights were out, we continued to talk. And sing. And eat.

The next day, Miss Ballard told me I could go home for a Christmas visit.

"You don't sound very happy about it," I said.

"I would prefer to keep you at the Sheltering Arms, where I can control your activities," she admitted. "You've made excellent progress, and you could undo it all by getting too tired or by trying to do something you aren't ready for and damaging a muscle." She shrugged. "But I don't have the heart to say no to your parents."

"I'll be careful," I promised. "I'm much stronger than I was on the first visit."

After days of practice with Miss Ballard, I could walk up a step or two. With luck, I'd be able to make it in the front door of my house on my own.

"Art will be home for the holidays," I told Miss Ballard. "He and Dad plan to make a chair out of their hands and carry me up and down the stairs so I can use the big bathroom and sleep in my own bed."

Miss Ballard clapped her hands over her ears and said she didn't want to know about it until after I was safely back at the Sheltering Arms.

I was not the only patient in 202 to receive a Christmas pass. Dorothy and Renée were going home, too. Shirley's parents and her two younger sisters were coming to spend Christmas Day with her; I was glad that she and Alice would have company.

Two days before we were scheduled to leave, Dorothy got pneumonia, and her visit home was canceled. She had trouble breathing, which scared all of us. We knew that if she got worse she would be moved to University Hospital and put back in an iron lung.

When my parents came to get me, my joy was marred by concern that when I returned, Dorothy might be gone. All of my roommates now seemed like sisters, and I desperately wanted Dorothy to get well. And I wanted her to stay at the Sheltering Arms with me.

This time, my visit went smoothly. I was able to keep my balance in the car, and I managed the front steps on my own. Grandpa had tears in his eyes as he held the door open and watched me walk in with my sticks, but I knew they were tears of happiness.

My only real difficulty was B.J., who was so glad to see me that he kept wagging around my ankles. We all worried that I would trip over him or that he would knock one of my sticks out of my hand. Dad wanted to shut B.J. in the basement.

"If B.J. has to go to the basement," I said, "I'm going with him."

B.J. was allowed to stay near me, but I spent a lot of time sitting down just so my dog wouldn't get in trouble.

Because I was stronger and able to move more easily, I didn't get so tired on this second visit. I wore my new plaid satin dress and sat in my usual place on the sofa for our Christmas Eve gift exchange. I gave Grandpa, Art, Mother, and Dad fancy Christmas cards I had made in O.T. I felt like one of the family again.

When it was time to go to bed, Mother carried my walking sticks up the stairs. Art and Dad made the "chair" out of their hands, I sat down and held on to their necks, and up we went. It worked fine, but I was glad Miss Ballard wasn't there to watch.

At the top of the stairs, Mother gave me my sticks and I walked eagerly into my own bedroom. Or was it my own bedroom? I stood in the doorway, totally stunned.

"Surprise!" Mother said.

"Merry Christmas!" Dad said.

They had completely redecorated my room. The walls and furniture had been painted, and a new white bedspread covered my bed. Ruffled curtains now framed the windows, and a new lamp shone from the bedside table.

I could barely hide my disappointment. I had thought a hundred times about my comfortable room with its worn bedspread and familiar furniture. I had longed to see it all again, and now that room was gone forever. Even the closet was clean.

"Wow," I said, trying to act thrilled. The redone bedroom seemed less like my own than Room 202 did, and I fell asleep wondering how Dorothy was.

In the morning, I decided I liked my new room, and that evening I left reluctantly for the Sheltering Arms. It had been good to be home again, and I had gotten around fairly well. Still, I knew I had a ways to go before I was well enough to come home for good. For one thing, Dad and Art would not be there all the time to carry me up and down the stairs.

I braced myself for bad news as I entered Room 202. Much to my relief, Dorothy was sitting up in bed, looking well.

"Look!" she said, the minute I arrived. She held her arm toward me. "My great-aunt in Montana sent me a watch!" Dorothy's parents were extremely poor, and she said she had never dreamed she would have a watch of her own. "She sent me a new dress, too," Dorothy said. "As soon as I'm well enough to get up, I'll wear it."

That night, the five of us talked long after lights out. Renée told what she had done at home. Shirley told about the visit from her parents and sisters.

"My mom came," Dorothy said, "and my brother who is on leave from the army." Even Alice had some exciting news: an uncle had come on Christmas Day to visit her.

After all of December's festivities, January seemed as dull as last month's newspapers. The days were short, and so were our tempers. Shirley caught a cold and had to stay in bed. Dorothy was over the pneumonia, but her braces didn't fit properly. They were returned and a new pair ordered. Even with new O.T. projects and another edition of the *Clutch*, the hospital newsletter, we were bored and restless.

Despite blizzards and icy roads, Mother and Dad came every Sunday. On one trip, Mother told me she had visited the little kids' ward.

"They don't have enough toys for those children," she said. "Little ones can't read to entertain themselves, the way you can."

I sensed that she was leading up to something, and I was right.

"I was thinking," she went on, "that you have outgrown many of your toys, and maybe you would like to donate them to the Sheltering Arms."

"Like what?" I asked.

"Your table and chairs, for one thing. You're much too big to fit in the chairs anymore, and they're just taking up space at home."

I agreed to donate my table and chairs.

"And your dolls. You haven't played with dolls for years, and there aren't enough dolls for all the children in that ward."

"Not my Raggedys," I said. "And not Marilyn or the Story Book Dolls. But you can give the rest away."

Mother nodded. "What about all your books? The little children would enjoy looking at the pictures."

I hesitated. I couldn't use the table and chairs even if I wanted to, and I didn't mind giving away the dolls as long as I got to keep my favorites. But my books? I felt sorry for the little kids, too, but there were limits to my generosity.

Apparently there were no limits to Mother's. "You haven't read those kiddie books in years," she pointed out. "Your health is improving so quickly, and some of the children in that ward are badly crippled." She made me feel like a selfish ogre.

"I want to keep my Raggedy Ann books," I said.

"Fine," she said. "I'll pack up all the rest."

I wanted to keep my other books, too, but I didn't have the nerve to say so. How could I complain about giving away *Donkey, Donkey* when I had not looked at it in five years?

The next Sunday, the car bulged with my belongings. In addition to dolls, books, and the table and chairs, Mother brought every toy in good condition that I hadn't played with in recent memory. There were balls, boxes of crayons, stuffed animals, and games. She even brought my doll buggy, the one I used to push Raggedy Ann in.

"Some little girl who can't yet walk alone might be able to walk by holding on to your buggy," Mother said.

I wanted to protest, but I could not dispute the facts: I was too big for that doll buggy, and most of the kids in the children's ward were worse off than I was.

Mother had a wonderful time distributing everything to the youngsters in the children's ward. Then, glowing with pride in her unselfish daughter, she told everyone it was all my idea.

Although my parents set a generous example, I never got any pleasure from watching the little kids use my possessions. Every time I saw my doll buggy or my maple table and chairs, I thought of home and how uncomplicated life used to be. When I saw a little boy reading *Donkey, Donkey*, I fought the urge to grab it away from him and hide it under my bed.

17: A Present for Dr. Bevis

"Stand up straight," Miss Ballard said.

As I practiced with my walking sticks, she kept reminding me of my posture. "Keep your shoulders back. Eyes ahead. Don't look down."

Each week I used my walking sticks more confidently, but I tended to hunch forward and watch the floor. Weak muscles made it difficult to keep my shoulders back, and I looked down all the time because I was afraid I would trip.

One morning, Miss Ballard brought a book to my physical therapy session. I recognized it; it was the bird identification book that was kept near the window in the classroom.

"This is how fashion models learn to stand straight," Miss Ballard told me as she placed the book on my head.

"They balance a book on their head and try not to drop it while they walk down the runway."

"It's heavy," I said.

"You're lucky I didn't bring an unabridged dictionary. Let's see how far you can get before it falls."

With *Birds of North America* perched on my head, I started across the room.

"Good! Good!" exclaimed Miss Ballard. "You look like a fashion model."

It was hard to keep the book from sliding off my head while I walked, especially after I began a running commentary, mimicking the only fashion show I had ever attended, a mother-daughter event at the Methodist church.

"Our next model is Peg," I said, "wearing a stunning blue sweatshirt and corduroy pants. Note the exquisite stains on her shirt front, done by a special process called spilled spaghetti. The stylish lump in the left sleeve is achieved with a wadded-up Kleenex. Doesn't Peg look gorgeous for a day of physical therapy?"

One memorable morning in late January, Miss Ballard said, "Today you're going to walk a few steps without your sticks."

My heart beat faster.

"Stand here," she said, motioning to a stretch of wall with a sturdy railing, "and hold on to the handrail."

I moved into position, handed her my walking sticks, and grasped the rail. She stood a few feet ahead of me.

"Slowly," she warned. "Heel first, then toe. Don't thump your whole foot down at once."

I nodded.

"If you have trouble, grab the rail."

I nodded again.

She smiled. "Let go of the rail," she said.

I did, too nervous even to tease her by suggesting I might sprint away.

She stretched her hands toward me. "Peg," she said, her voice hushed, "you're going to walk."

I licked my lips and stared at her.

"Now," she whispered.

Carefully, I raised one foot and set it down a few inches in front of me. My arms prickled with excitement.

"Heel," Miss Ballard said, "then toe. Small steps."

Wobbling slightly, I moved the other foot. I held my arms a few inches away from my body to help me balance.

"Head up. Don't look down. Shoulders back. Pretend you have the book on your head."

I took another small, unsteady step.

"Heel," she said. "Toe. Heel. Toe." With each word, the excitement in her voice intensified.

Head up, staring at Miss Ballard, I walked. I walked!

Six steps later, my hands grasped hers, and we celebrated our mutual victory with a hug.

"You still need the walking sticks most of the time," she warned, as she handed them to me. "Don't try to walk alone unless I'm with you."

"Who, me?" I said.

"I mean it, Peg. No walking by yourself." She put her hands on her hips. "And no hula dancing, either."

"How did you know about that?"

I followed her instructions faithfully. I had come too far, at too great a cost, to risk a setback. Besides, I could get around faster with my sticks than I could on my own. Walking unaided slowed me down.

From then on, I practiced walking alone for a short time each day. With Miss Ballard barking directions like an army drill sergeant, I heeled and toed my way around the physical therapy room. Gradually, I gained assurance.

I still had to concentrate on each step, but my gait grew smoother and the steps I took became more normal in length.

While I learned to walk by myself, Dorothy struggled to walk using both her new braces and her walking sticks. She tried hard, knowing that if she could not manage, she would always be in a wheelchair.

Renée made more progress than Dorothy did. She needed help getting her leg braces on, but once she was on her feet she could move about with her walking sticks.

On a frigid February morning, Miss Ballard watched me walk alone and said, "How would you like to go home?"

"You mean, for good?"

"Yes. I've done all I can for you. From now on, you only need to continue your exercises and practice walking alone. Go a few steps farther each day without your sticks, the way we've been doing here. I know your parents will help you, and I think you want to help yourself."

I nodded, not trusting myself to speak.

"The doctors have already agreed to your discharge," she went on. "All we have to do is notify your parents that they can come and get you."

Home. I was going home.

"You'll need to come back for checkups," Miss Ballard told me. "Every week at first, and then every month. We have to be sure you continue to make progress."

"It'll be fun to come back; I'll want to see the other kids."

"They're going to miss you," she said. "We all will."

"I'll miss you, too," I said, and I threw my arms around her.

On my last night at the Sheltering Arms, I passed out all the food from under my bed, declaring I didn't want to haul it home with me. Feeling like my mother's daughter, I gave away my stationery and pen, my hand mirror, my back scratcher, and even my teddy bear, insisting that each of the girls keep something of mine to remember me by.

"We won't miss you," Renée teased, "but we'll sure miss your parents."

"And your food," said Alice.

My emotions were a roller coaster, rocketing to elation that I would soon be home to stay and then plunging to sadness at the thought of leaving my friends.

That night, we sang every song we had ever done,

even the Christmas carols. We sang and sang and sang, with the music floating over the five beds and disappearing into our memories.

Mother arrived at ten the next morning. I was glad she came early. Once the day of departure had come, I did not want to linger. Even so, the good-byes were hard to say. They were made bearable only by the fact that I had to return for a checkup the following week and promised to bring a full report from the outside world.

"Never mind the report," said Renée. "Just bring potato chips."

Her humor chased our nostalgia out the door, and I followed.

"Good-bye!" the girls called. "Good-bye! Don't forget to write!"

Miss Ballard saw me to the car, spouting instructions for Mother and reminders for me.

While Mother laid my walking sticks across the back seat, I hugged Miss Ballard. "Thank you," I said. "See you next week."

"No running," Miss Ballard warned as she closed the car door for me. "No funny tricks. No hula."

While Mother got in the driver's side, I rolled down my window.

"Is it okay," I asked Miss Ballard, "if I try out my old roller skates?"

"You'll do nothing of the kind," Mother said.

"I don't want to hear about it," Miss Ballard said, but she smiled at me as she covered her ears.

"We have to stop at University Hospital before we go home," I told Mother. "I promised Dr. Bevis I'd come back and walk for him."

"I know," she said. "I brought him a present."

Somehow, that didn't surprise me.

Once more, I rode from the Sheltering Arms to University Hospital. This time I didn't have to pretend I was dead.

"I wasn't sure what to get Dr. Bevis," Mother said, "so I bought him a necktie. I hope he's there today."

He was. We waited in the lobby while he was paged, and he greeted us warmly.

"I see you've graduated to walking sticks," he told me. "No more wheelchair."

"We're on our way home," Mother told him. "Peg was discharged today."

"That's wonderful news."

"We brought you a present," I said. Mother gave him the box.

When he saw the tie, he said, "It's beautiful. I'll think of you whenever I wear it."

"I have something to show you," I said as I handed my walking sticks to Mother.

Then, smiling triumphantly at Dr. Bevis, I walked across the hospital lobby to the information desk, turned, and walked back again. Head up, shoulders back; heel, toe, heel, toe. Small steps.

Dr. Bevis watched closely. "You did it!" he said. "You can walk!"

I stopped in front of him, standing straight. "Thank you for helping me," I said.

He took both my hands in his, looking as if he had just won the lottery. "Thank you for coming to show me."

Mother gave me my sticks, and Dr. Bevis went to the door with us. "Good-bye, Peg," he said. "I'm proud of you."

A necktie and two minutes of watching a young girl walk alone. I hope it was adequate payment for all he had given me.

18: Back to School

When we got home this time, I was no longer a visitor, and we soon settled into a routine. Mornings were exercise time. The first day, Mother opened a paper bag and dumped a pile of marbles on the floor in front of me.

"Miss Ballard said you would know what to do," she told me.

After my exercises, I practiced walking without my sticks. I decided to practice with a book on my head. Twice each day, I walked alone until I grew tired, trying to go one minute longer every session.

The rest of the time, I used my sticks. Because they stuck out on each side, it was harder to walk with them at home than it had been at the Sheltering Arms. Even though Mother and Dad pushed the furniture against the walls, I had less room to maneuver. Still, I was in no hurry to discard my sticks. I felt far more secure with them than I did when I walked alone, and they kept me from becoming too tired.

Every afternoon, I studied. Without the distraction of four roommates, I did my lessons quickly. But I worried that I might be far behind my classmates. What if I didn't pass those final exams?

I was allowed one visitor each day, for fifteen minutes. My friends took turns coming, but the visits seemed strained. Although we were genuinely glad to see each other, they could not help staring at my walking sticks. Instead of giving me news from school, they wanted to hear what it was like to have polio.

"Did it hurt?" they asked. "Were you really paralyzed from the neck down?" "Did you almost die?"

What will it be like, I worried, when I go back to school? Will everyone stare? Will kids I don't even know want to hear the details of my time in the hospital? I felt like a freak in a sideshow, valued only because I was different.

A week after my discharge, we returned to the Sheltering Arms for my first checkup. Miss Ballard was pleased with my progress. I could hardly wait to see the other girls and catch up on all the hospital news.

When we went up to Room 202, Dorothy, Renée, and Alice were in school, and a new girl was in my bed. I talked awhile with Shirley and left, feeling disappointed and slightly resentful that life at the Sheltering Arms was rolling smoothly along without me.

My second checkup was scheduled at one o'clock, so we went early and visited in Room 202 while the girls ate lunch.

During my first weeks at home, I frequently sat by the window and watched for the mailman, hoping for news from the Sheltering Arms. I wrote regularly to Room 202. Renée and Dorothy wrote back often; Alice wrote occasionally. Shirley could not write by herself, but the letters from the other girls always said, "P.S. Shirley says to tell you hi."

Oddly, I didn't listen to the "Lone Ranger" after I went home. Tonto and Silver now belonged to a different part of my life.

After four checkups, Miss Ballard said I didn't need to come back for a month. When I arrived that time, Dorothy said, "I won't be here the next time you come. I'm going home on Saturday."

"Did the new braces work?" I asked.

Dorothy shook her head, no. "My brothers are building a ramp so I can get in and out of our house."

I was glad that she was going home, and sad that she would always need the wheelchair.

When it was time for us to leave, I hugged Dorothy, wondering if I would ever see her again. We promised to write often, and that promise held back my tears.

We had good intentions, but letters between me and my roommates slowed, in both directions. There were two new girls in 202 now.

About two weeks after she was discharged, I got a letter from Dorothy. "I wanted to leave Sheltering Arms more than anything," she wrote, "but now sometimes I wish I could go back. Isn't that silly?"

It wasn't silly to me. We were safe at the Sheltering Arms, cocooned in Room 202, where everyone understood what it was like to have polio. Getting around in the normal world, even in our own homes, was more difficult than hospital life.

In April, I got permission to return to school. I was still on my walking sticks, but I could go up and down stairs if I held the railing with both hands and had someone carry my sticks for me. I was slow because both feet had to touch every step, but I could make it.

Dad bought me a backpack for my books. I was to start by attending only in the mornings. If I could manage that, I would gradually work up to a full day.

On my first day back, I was so nervous my hands began to sweat and I was afraid the sticks would slip out of my grasp. What if people never quit staring? What if no one would carry my sticks up and down stairs for me? What if I couldn't get around in the crowded halls, and fell? Worst of all, what if I discovered that I was hopelessly behind the other kids in every class?

When I walked into my first-period class, which happened to be English, the students whistled and clapped and cheered, welcoming me back. All morning, kids begged for a turn to carry my sticks up or down the stairs. They offered to help me with the backpack. They walked ahead of me in the halls, clearing space.

Without knowing it, I had become a celebrity. Since I was the only person in Austin to get polio that year, the whole town had followed my progress while I was in the hospital. It seems all of Austin had been pulling for me, hoping I would walk again.

Rather than falling behind in my classes, it quickly became clear that I had remained equal or even pulled slightly ahead. By the end of the morning, I felt sure that I would pass the final exams.

My last class of the morning was chorus practice. Thanks to all those songs in the dark, my singing voice was improved, even though I now used my stomach muscles rather than my diaphragm.

As I found my seat and placed my sticks on the floor beside me, I remembered how my skirt had jumped because of my twitching thigh muscle on Homecoming day, and how I had collapsed in the hall when chorus ended.

I had been gone seven months. I had been gone a lifetime. Although I returned on walking sticks, moving slowly and taking small steps, I knew that in many ways, I was stronger than when I left.

I opened my music and began to sing.

Epilogue

Within a year of leaving the Sheltering Arms, I was able to walk without the sticks, attend school full-time, and lead a nearly normal life. I graduated from Austin High School and spent a year at the University of Minnesota.

Peg Schulze became Peg Kehret when I married my best friend, Carl Kehret. I wept for joy the day our children, Anne and Bob, got their first polio vaccinations.

My dream of being a writer never faded. I wrote short stories, magazine articles, plays, and adult books before discovering that what I like best is writing books for young people. I have published forty-three books; all but two are for children. Perhaps I like to write from the viewpoint of a twelve- or thirteen-year-old because I remember that time in my life so clearly.

Although I never became a veterinarian, animals enliven

most of my books. I volunteer for animal welfare causes, and because I had the good sense to marry a man who loved animals, I've always shared my home with various rescued creatures. For many years, Carl and I took two cats and a dog along in our motor home when we traveled across the United States for my talks at schools and library conventions.

Through the years, I corresponded with my roommates.

Dorothy was carried, in her wheelchair, up and down the school steps each day until she graduated from high school. She got married, had seven children, and now has eighteen grandchildren and eight great-grandchildren! Until she retired, she was the senior receptionist at Courage Center in Minneapolis, a rehabilitation center for people with physical disabilities.

Renée also finished high school and led an active life. For many years, she wrote a weekly column for her local newspaper, and she researched and wrote a history of her church. Renée's condition worsened in mid-life until, unable to live on her own, she moved to a care center. Even living in such a restricted situation, Renée never lost her sense of humor or her zest for life. One year her

Christmas letter was written from the viewpoint of her bed!

Alice, too, graduated from high school, then moved to a home for adults with disabilities. She was secretary for the United Handicapped Federation in St. Paul, Minnesota, and sang in a church choir. Long after Alice grew up and moved away from the Sheltering Arms, her older brother decided to search for her. He remembered the little sister who went to the hospital and never returned, and after his parents died, he found her! Although Alice continued to live in the group home, this brother and his wife visited her and took her to their home for holiday dinners. So in the end, Alice had some family of her own. Alice died of cancer in 1993.

Shirley lost her battle with polio. She died in 1955, just five years after our time together.

Ten years have passed since *Small Steps* was published. When the book first came out, Dorothy, Renée, and I had a "polio reunion." Carl and I drove to Minnesota, and Dorothy and her husband met us at the care center where Renée lived. We spent a happy day reminiscing about our time together at the Sheltering Arms.

Renée died in 2005. Dorothy and I still keep in touch.

My brother, Art, graduated from Carleton College and Harvard Business School. He had a business career with General Mills, retiring as executive vice president. Art married and has four children and seven grandchildren. He is now tall, gray, and handsome.

My mother and father are gone now, but Mother was alive when *Small Steps* was first published, and she enjoyed giving copies to all of her friends. My parents were remarkable people, and I'm pleased that their memory lives on in the minds of readers who never met them.

Tommy, my "Lone Ranger" buddy, disappeared from my life after I left University Hospital. I never found out if he got weaned from the iron lung or not. I don't remember Tommy's last name, and without that there is no way to trace him.

I've been asked by several readers why I didn't visit Tommy on the day I walked for Dr. Bevis at University Hospital. There's a simple answer: I was not there on a day that had visiting hours, which were strictly enforced.

Perhaps someone who reads *Small Steps* will know who Tommy was, and will contact me. I know it could happen because that's how I found Dr. Bevis.

When I was writing *Small Steps*, I was not able to

locate Dr. Bevis. University Hospital, where I was his patient, no longer had information about him; there was no listing for him in the Minneapolis or St. Paul telephone directory; and the Internet was not yet a common means of searching for someone.

After the book was published, I received a letter from a school librarian. She told me that a few years earlier she had given birth to a premature baby and had been helped by "a marvelous older doctor" named Dr. Bevis. She wondered if it might be the same man.

I contacted the librarian to learn where she had lived when her baby was born, then I found a telephone number for *Bevis* in that area. When Dr. Bevis answered, I inquired if he had been an intern at University Hospital in Minneapolis, and he said, "Yes." I was talking to MY Dr. Bevis!

After I explained who I was and why I was calling, we had a long conversation. He told me of his early work with polio patients at the Sister Kenny Institute in Minneapolis, followed by many years as a pediatrician. I learned about his wife and his four children, and I told him about my husband and family. He asked about my parents, for he remembered them.

I sent him copies of the book and after he read it, he wrote to thank me. We have corresponded occasionally ever since. In one letter he told me that he once had a date with Sister Kenny! Because we live at opposite sides of the United States we have not renewed our friendship in person, but I am glad to know that he had a successful career and a happy marriage.

As I wait to learn someday about Tommy, I also hope that a reader will recognize Miss Ballard and put me in touch with her. I've been told that she married and moved to the East Coast, but I don't know her married name or where she went to live.

Since there is a photo of Miss Ballard in the book and because I do know her first name (Althea), I hold out hope that I will eventually find her.

I've made dozens of new friends as a result of this book. Many are polio survivors who write to tell me how similar their experiences were to mine and to thank me for putting our history on paper.

Patricia of Schenectady, New York, got polio five years after I did, when she was a freshman in college. She didn't have a bear, but she did have a stuffed monkey named Jojo, who had a head made of some hard substance.

When Pat came out of isolation, the nurse cut off Jojo's head, washed it with alcohol, and gave it to Pat. Only the blue and yellow body got burned.

Pat also wrote, "I was told to push the call button if I couldn't breathe anymore. That was a fine idea, but I couldn't reach the button when I tried, so I decided that I'd better just keep on breathing."

Although Pat was hospitalized for only one month, she remembers that her mother sent the doctor a Thanksgiving card every year for the rest of her life.

Dorothy Young, who had polio at age eleven in Arkansas, never made a complete recovery but managed to raise five children and to accomplish things that she shouldn't have been able to do at all. Dorothy shared a secret with me: "I've watched runners accepting their awards after marathon races on television, and thought to myself, I run my own kind of marathon almost daily. I've awarded myself a heap of imaginary medals along the way."

Dorothy's attitude is typical of the polio survivors I've met or corresponded with. They have a determination to make the most of their lives, regardless of any lasting handicaps.

Some letters made me weep. Bev Jennings of Belle-vue, Washington, told me that her brother, Walt, died of bulbar polio in September 1948. He was only twelve.

Bev majored in biology in college. After she gradu-ated in 1954, she worked for Parke-Davis, a drug com-pany, where she spent four years doing safety testing of the Salk polio vaccine. She wrote, "I am ever grateful to Jonas Salk and his workers for all they achieved. It wasn't soon enough for my brother and you and many others, but thanks to their persistence, and later the work of Dr. Sabin, polio was conquered."

Audrey of Detroit, Michigan, got polio in 1939, before the Sister Kenny treatments were available. She had casts on both legs for a month but eventually went to a chil-dren's convalescent hospital where she got therapy in a heated pool. It took more than five years for Audrey to fully recover.

"It might sound strange," Audrey says of her time in the hospital, "but those were happy days. We went to school every day. Entertainers would come out. I learned to swim."

I wasn't the only polio patient who formed friendships with her roommates. Audrey still remembers all the girls who were with her in the hospital. They used to sing together when music was piped into their ward.

No matter what age my fellow survivors were when they had polio, or how well they recovered, everyone who got the Sister Kenny treatments agrees on one point: we all hated the hot packs! Letter after letter echoes my description of the steaming wool cloths and tells how much the patients dreaded them. Everyone disliked the exercises, too, and they agreed with my name of Torture Time.

Shirley Perry of Orleans, Vermont, was six when she got polio in 1949, the same year I got sick. Instead of being hospitalized, Shirley was kept at home and treated with hot packs there. She remembers wondering why her kind, wonderful mother was burning her.

Don from Udall, Kansas, remembers screaming when his mother raised his tight legs over his head as she did his therapy exercises after he was released from the hospital. How hard it must have been for loving parents to know that the only way to help their children recover the use of their muscles would cause those children great pain.

Many people wrote to say they, too, had been a polio

patient at Sheltering Arms. Barbara Hulsingh of Edgewood, Washington, even remembers Alice!

Barbara arrived at Sheltering Arms three years after I went home. By then I was in high school, walking unassisted, working on the school newspaper and yearbook, and acting in school plays. I had met my future husband. Life's possibilities stretched before me like an unending road and I raced forward with exuberance and anticipation, while Alice remained at Sheltering Arms in the same physical condition as when I left, except for being three years older. Once again I realized how fortunate I was.

Pat Hofmaster of Sacramento, California, was a polio patient at Sheltering Arms in 1953. A senior executive with the American Red Cross, Pat exemplifies the determination of most polio survivors. She wrote, "Polio left me with paralysis in my left arm. . . . In spite of having to figure out some unique ways of physically doing things, I have led canoe trips on Lake Superior, annually back-pack in Mexico and Central America, enjoy my foot-pedal kayak, and look forward to the next adventure."

Every one of the polio survivors who wrote to me (and I had room to mention only a small percentage of them here) is a person I would enjoy spending time with.

There were no cries of "Life isn't fair!" Even those with severe problems sought only to exchange information. There wasn't a whiner in the bunch.

Teachers told me about classroom projects that they did after reading *Small Steps*. Jo Auchterlonie, a fifth-grade teacher in Wichita, Kansas, borrowed two wheelchairs and let her students sign up to spend half a day in one of them.

The students wrote to tell me of their experience. "We thought it would be fun," they said, "but it was hard. Our arms ached. We were slow. We couldn't get into the bathroom if someone else wanted to come out, and we couldn't sit with our friends. Sitting at a desk wasn't always comfortable, and using a clipboard was worse."

Several students have asked me if I ever found out how I got polio. There is no way to solve that mystery. Probably I got it from someone who had such a mild case that they didn't even know they had polio.

Many teachers showed their students the 1998 PBS special about polio, "A Paralyzing Fear," which is available as a video or DVD, and several played "Lone Ranger" tapes for their classes. One innovative teacher had her wiggly fourth-grade boys lie on the floor and pretend to be paralyzed while she read to them. Another invited a polio survivor to talk to the students and give them a tour of her special van with its wheelchair lift and hand controls.

As teachers strengthened their students' empathy toward people with disabilities, *Small Steps* led to some unexpected strengthening of family ties. Many grandparents reported being invited to visit their grandchild's school to share their polio experiences, often stating that they had never before discussed this with their family.

Other gratifying letters came from people who told me that reading *Small Steps* helped them cope in their current struggle with some other problem. One nine-year-old girl had been home from school with a painful case of shingles for five months and claimed the book made her determined to get well.

Greg Immethun of Lees Summit, Missouri, broke his neck when he was eighteen and was paralyzed from the neck down at first, but eventually regained about half of his original strength. He told me the book helped him release some of the pent-up emotions that he had locked inside at the time of his injury, twenty-four years earlier.

Greg wrote, "You said that you are in an exclusive sorority of people who have had polio. I hope you know that it also includes anybody who has been through a life-changing injury like ours was."

A different kind of nonpolio letter came from Ken Ptomey of Pittsburgh, Pennsylvania. Ken was a forty-six-year-old grandfather who was learning to read as a student at Greater Pittsburgh Literacy Council. *Small Steps* was the first book Ken ever read.

When he finished it, he wrote to tell me of his struggles as an adult literacy student. He said, "I am able to identify with your physical disability and your strength because of my pain of learning how to read. It's a disability for me when I trip and stumble through words, and through your book I feel hope."

Time after time, such unexpected tributes lifted my spirits, gave me motivation to continue writing, and made me feel that my life's work is worthwhile. Whatever these correspondents gained from reading *Small Steps*, they returned to me tenfold.

Forty years after the events of this book, I began to have muscle aches, foot cramps, back pain, and fatigue. Even more alarming, I began to lose strength in my arms and legs. I was shocked to learn that my problems were caused by my old adversary, polio.

The condition is called post-polio syndrome. Thousands of former polio patients, including Dorothy, are experiencing similar difficulties. Decades after their original illness, polio survivors are reluctantly returning to the walking sticks, braces, and wheelchairs that they fought so hard to be rid of.

For years I drew inner strength from my victory over polio, feeling that if I could beat polio, I could handle anything. It was painful to discover that the enemy was not vanquished, as I had thought, but had merely gone under cover, waiting to strike once more.

My battle with polio is not over.

As with the initial disease, there is no cure for post-polio syndrome. My muscles continue to get weaker, and I now use a cane when I'm away from my house. (My cane has cat faces all over it.) Because of fatigue and muscle pain, I've had to eliminate many activities that I used to enjoy, such as school talks.

Although my struggle with polio continues, I no longer have to endure Torture Time, or pick up marbles with my toes.

The physical problems are not as difficult to deal with as the emotional ones. Carl died in 2004; we had been married for forty-eight years. Like having polio, his death was a life-changing event that now affects every part of my existence.

Healing is a painful process, just as it was back in my polio days, but my family, friends, pets, and readers constantly give me reasons to celebrate what I still have.

Since Carl's death, I've taken many small steps toward creating a new life, by myself. I've written books, I've traveled to conferences to receive awards, and I continue to help animals. I don't feel the same unconditional joy that I used to feel, yet I am happy.

My main hobby is reading. I also enjoy pumping my player piano and browsing in antiques shops. I live in a log house on ten acres of forest near Mount Rainier National Park in Washington State. My property is a wildlife sanctuary where my four grandchildren love to watch for deer, elk, rabbits, and many kinds of birds.

My son, Bob, is a high school teacher who coaches volleyball and track. His wife, Pam, is also a teacher. My daughter, Anne, is a gymnastics coach and Girl Scout leader. Her husband, Kevin, has a video production company.

My grandchildren, Brett, Chelsea, Eric, and Mark, all have books dedicated to them, as do their parents.

Small Steps won many awards and honors. If I had to choose the one thing I'm most proud of that resulted from this book, it would be the many letters from children who said that because of *Small Steps* they appreciate their own good health and their loving families more than they used to.

They tell me they now understand what's truly important because I realized it when I was at Sheltering Arms, and later put my memories into words.

My sincere thanks for all the letters. I'm glad I shared my polio experiences with you.

Peg Kehret
March 2006

More about Polio

References to polio date back thousands of years. A stone carving made around 1500 B.C.E. shows a man named Ruma, a gatekeeper at an Egyptian temple, leaning on a staff. Ruma's right leg is smaller and shorter than the left, and his right foot points down in the "dropfoot" characteristic of polio.

Although the disease had not yet been named, cases of what must have been polio were also reported in ancient Greek and Roman times. The first clinical description was written by a British physician in 1789, but he still did not name the illness. Most cases of polio cause flu-like symptoms but do not cause death or paralysis. Until epidemics of paralytic polio began to occur, a century later, the disease got less attention than diseases such as diphtheria and smallpox.

In 1840, a German doctor named the disease "infantile paralysis" because victims were so often children. Eventually, the disease's scientific name would be poliomyelitis, but it is usually called polio.

In the late 1800s, the first recorded polio epidemics struck, in Scandinavia. In 1894, a small town in Vermont reported forty-four cases of paralytic polio, and in 1916, twenty-seven thousand cases were reported in the United States, with six thousand deaths. By then it was known that polio is caused by a virus, but no one knew how to keep the disease from spreading or how to treat those who contracted it. For the next forty years, major epidemics broke out each year in the U.S.

Ironically, scientists believe that improved sanitation caused the dramatic increase in polio. Until the beginning of the twentieth century, most infants acquired the poliovirus from unsanitary conditions, such as fecal material in the water supply. The babies were infected, but because they were still protected by antibodies from their mothers, their sickness was mild. (Antibodies are substances produced by the body's immune system that destroy or neutralize bacteria, viruses, or other harmful toxins.) The virus stimulated the babies' immune systems enough to produce their own antibodies, which gave them lifelong protection against polio.

Then health officials began keeping the water supply clean, and rules of hygiene such as washing one's hands before eating became widely known. While standards of cleanliness rose, so did the number of polio cases because now children were not exposed to the virus until long after the immunity that they got from their mothers had ended.

As polio increased, so did fear of the disease. During epidemics, public swimming pools closed, and children were barred from movie theaters so infection wouldn't spread. In the 1916 epidemic, officials in New York City, which had the most cases, thought that animals might spread the disease. They captured and killed seventy-two thousand stray cats. Towns near New York City placed signs on their main roads warning children from the city not to enter. Since the epidemics occurred during the summer months, some parents decided sunshine made children more vulnerable, so they allowed their children to go outdoors only after dark. Other children were required to wear gloves all summer, to keep germs off their hands.

None of these preventive efforts stopped the polio epidemics. Many victims died. Those who survived were often crippled for life. Their withered limbs, heavy metal braces, and wheelchairs were constant reminders of the devastation polio caused. People encased in iron lungs symbolized the terrible helplessness that parents felt as they feared for their children. For half a century, dread stalked American families. Children and adults, rich and poor, city dwellers and farmers—all feared the same unseen foe: polio.

The poliovirus attacks the nerve cells in the brain and spinal cord that control the muscles of the body. If damage to the nerve cells is slight, the muscle weakness will be temporary. If the virus kills many nerve cells, paralysis will be extensive and possibly permanent.

There is no cure for polio. There are no miracle medicines to stop the damage to nerve cells or repair those already damaged. Today's polio patients are still treated with moist heat and muscle-stretching exercises, just as I was over fifty years ago.

In 1921, Franklin Delano Roosevelt, aged thirty-nine, was diagnosed with polio. Roosevelt had run for vice president of the United States a year earlier, and although he lost that election, he was a popular public figure who anticipated a national political career. The best doctors confirmed his diagnosis but could not cure him or even suggest treatment. Roosevelt's legs were paralyzed.

He did not give up easily. Determined to regain the use of his legs, he spent seven years in rehabilitation, but despite his efforts, he never again walked without help.

Much of Roosevelt's rehab was done at Warm Springs, a spa in Georgia whose warm waters were said to cure paralysis. Although he wasn't cured, the buoyant water helped Roosevelt move better, swimming built up the strength in his upper body, and the exercise gave him a feeling of well-being.

In 1926, Roosevelt bought Warm Springs. The next year, he and his law partner, Basil O'Connor, made it a nonprofit foundation for polio survivors. In 1928, Roosevelt left Warm Springs to run for governor of New York.

Roosevelt went on to win four terms as president of the United States. Instead of leading the secluded life of an invalid, as expected at that time, he led the U.S. toward victory in World War II and out of the Great Depression. In those days, disabled people were perceived as weak and unable to contribute to society, so Roosevelt discouraged photographs of himself in his wheelchair. When he gave a speech, he wore hip-high leg braces and used a cane so that he could stand while he spoke.

To raise money to support its programs, the Warm Springs Foundation held "Birthday Balls" in eight cities on Roosevelt's birthday, January 30, 1934. The balls were so successful that they became an annual event, spreading to more locations each year.

In 1938, Roosevelt, then in his second term as president, established the National Foundation for Infantile Paralysis. With much fanfare, he announced that the new organization would finance investigation into the cause of polio and the methods by which it might be prevented. The National Foundation would also pay for patient care.

Eddie Cantor, a famous entertainer, suggested a new kind of fund-raiser, aimed not at the wealthy few who attended balls but at the masses of ordinary citizens who, fearing for the safety of their children, wanted to defeat polio. Cantor coined the phrase "The March of Dimes" and urged people to send their dimes directly to the White House. Mailbags full of silver coins soon arrived in

Washington, D.C.—a total of two million, six hundred eighty thousand dimes in the first few months! That method of fund-raising continued, and was so successful that eventually the foundation's official name was changed to the March of Dimes.

Celebrities such as Willie Mays, Lucille Ball, and Frank Sinatra championed the cause. Movies were stopped partway through while volunteers from local March of Dimes chapters passed collection plates, asking people to donate their change.

Each year a few children who had polio were chosen to be photographed, and the photos were made into posters that were widely displayed.

In 1946, a biographical movie, *Sister Kenny* starring Rosalind Russell, took the country by storm. It increased the fear of polio and also the determination to find a way to prevent it. (Years later, my husband and I rented this film, but I couldn't bear to watch it. An early scene of a young girl in pain and unable to move her legs left me tearful and shaking.)

As more and more men went overseas to fight in World War II, women took over the important volunteer positions with the March of Dimes. In 1950, a group of women in Phoenix, Arizona, organized a Mothers' March on Polio. On the night of the Mothers' March, anyone who wanted to contribute money to fight polio was asked to turn on their porch light at seven o'clock. The marching mothers would knock only at dwellings whose outdoor lights were on.

The Phoenix moms raised $45,000 that night, and a year later the first national Mothers' March on Polio was held. By then rumors of a possible vaccine were creating excitement and enthusiasm for the cause. Throughout the country, hundreds of volunteers stood ready to go, and at seven o'clock church bells rang, fire stations blew their sirens, and motorists honked their horns—all to remind everyone that it was time to turn on the light and contribute to the fight against polio. Children accompanied their parents to help collect funds.

On the evening of that Mothers' March, I had been home from the hospital for nearly a year. My mother was one of the marchers, and I walked beside her. There were no dark porches in my neighborhood that night; every home blazed with light.

The fund-raising escalated, but so did the polio epidemics. Year after year, thousands of people were afflicted. The worst year, 1952, brought 57,879 cases. During one horrible five-day period, doctors diagnosed 4,191 cases of polio.

Hospital staffs were overwhelmed; patients shared rooms intended for one person, and the panic over polio increased.

The cost of care was astronomical. My parents had used up their savings and remortgaged their house, yet they still couldn't pay all my hospital bills. Some families had more than one child with polio; sometimes a parent was stricken. The March of Dimes funded all of this patient care, including mine after my parents ran out of funds. Not only did the March of Dimes pay hospital bills, but it purchased iron lungs and other medical equipment and established rehabilitation centers. It also funded scientists as they hunted for a way to prevent polio.

While the epidemics raged and the public contributed money, researchers worked to develop a polio vaccine. By the late 1940s, scientists knew that the poliovirus enters the body through the mouth, goes into the digestive system, then to the bloodstream, and finally to the nervous system, where it attacks the cells that tell the muscles what to do.

The principle of immunization was also known: inject a body with a small amount of disease in order to stimulate that body's immune system to produce antibodies to fight the disease. The trick was to create enough antibodies without creating a severe form of the disease.

Getting enough poliovirus to work with was difficult, too, as it was grown in the nerve tissue of live monkeys. It was time-consuming to extract the virus from the monkey tissue, and only tiny amounts of virus could be produced. Since the monkeys were killed before the tissue was taken, more monkeys were always necessary. Scientists needed a way to grow the virus in large quantities outside of living animals.

Early experiments failed. Then three scientists in Boston discovered how to grow poliovirus in cells in test tubes instead of in live monkeys, which enabled researchers to produce enough virus to make large quantities of vaccine. These scientists, John F. Enders, Frederick C. Robbins, and Thomas H. Weller, won the 1954 Nobel Prize in Medicine for their important discovery.

A difference of opinion developed among the leading researchers about whether the vaccine should be made from inactive, or killed, virus or from a weakened live virus. Dr. Jonas Salk, who had produced flu vaccines from a killed virus, used that method in his efforts to produce a polio vaccine.

Dr. Albert Sabin preferred a live but weakened virus, a method that had succeeded against rabies and smallpox. The efforts of both men were funded by the March of Dimes.

Dr. Salk's vaccine was ready for human trial first. His faith in it was so great that he injected himself, his wife, and his three sons before he gave it to the public. Lab workers who worked on the vaccine also voluntarily took the injections. No one suffered bad effects, and their bodies' immune systems produced polio antibodies, as Dr. Salk had hoped.

In 1954, Dr. Salk was ready for a massive field trial with healthy children from all across the country. By participating in this trial, one million, eight hundred thousand children became "Polio Pioneers." They each received a certificate and a tin Polio Pioneer button to wear. They were divided into three groups: some received the vaccine, some got injections containing no vaccine, and some simply had their health monitored for comparison.

It was a huge undertaking. Along with all the doctors and nurses, some fifty thousand teachers and over two hundred thousand volunteers were on hand to help. Computers were not much in use yet, so it took a long time for all the data to be recorded, collected, and analyzed. Later, records of polio cases from that summer were compared with the records of the children who actually received the vaccine.

The field trial took place in the spring and summer of 1954, but the results were not known until the spring of 1955. At ten A.M. on April 12, 1955, the tenth anniversary of Franklin Delano Roosevelt's death, the announcement electrified the world: the Salk vaccine was safe and effective!

I was a student at the University of Minnesota that spring. When I heard the news on the radio, my emotions churned. Elation that polio could be prevented wrestled with regret that I had missed the vaccine by only six years. By five-thirty that afternoon, the federal government had licensed the manufacture of polio vaccine. Jonas Salk instantly became a national hero. When asked who owned the patent on his vaccine, he replied, "Well, the people I would say. There is no patent. Could you patent the sun?"

Within two years, the number of polio cases in the United States dropped by 80 percent.

In 1959, five years after Dr. Salk's successful trial, Dr. Sabin was ready to test his live-virus vaccine, which was taken by mouth. A field trial required a large population that had not yet been vaccinated. By this time the Salk vaccine had been widely used in the U.S., so Sabin's trial was held in Russia, with ten million children vaccinated. It, too, was successful. In 1962, the oral vaccine was approved for use in the U.S. and soon replaced the injected Salk vaccine as the preferred method because it was cheaper and easier to administer.

Like Dr. Salk, Dr. Sabin did not patent his vaccine. While both men could easily have become millionaires, they chose instead to make their life-saving discoveries available for the public good.

The last case of naturally occurring polio in the U.S. was in 1979, but each year a few people got vaccine-associated polio because their immune systems were not strong enough to fight off the low dose of live virus in the vaccine. In 1998, a group of parents whose children had contracted polio this way petitioned the Centers for Disease Control, a government agency responsible for preventing infectious and chronic diseases, asking that the use of the live virus vaccine be stopped. In 2000, the U.S. again began using only vaccine made with the inactivated virus.

Vaccination programs were so successful that in 1994, polio was declared eliminated in the Western hemisphere, although occasional cases are diagnosed in families who refuse vaccination.

In 1985—thirty years after the licensing of the Salk vaccine—Rotary International, a service organization, made the worldwide eradication of polio its top goal. Rotarians raised millions of dollars to buy vaccine and the equipment to distribute it; they recruited volunteers from all around the world to carry out the task.

Three years later, the World Health Organization joined the effort. Soon the United Nations International Children's Emergency Fund and the Centers for Disease Control signed on. Those four organizations have continued to work together to stamp out polio. It is the largest public health initiative the world has ever known. On a single day in 2001, one hundred fifty million children in India were immunized.

In 1988, 350,000 cases of polio were reported worldwide. By 2005, that number had dropped to 1882. Ninety percent of those cases were in Nigeria, India, and Pakistan. The World Health Organization has declared the western Pacific and Europe free of polio and in February 2006, announced that Egypt is now polio-free.

In underdeveloped countries, it takes months of preparation before the vaccine can be given. Children must first be counted so authorities know how much vaccine is needed. A plan must be drawn up for how to get the vaccine to them.

Timing is crucial because the vaccine has to be kept cold—a huge challenge in areas where there is no refrigeration. People in remote villages who have never received any kind of health care often must be persuaded in advance to allow their children to receive the vaccine. There may be no roads; many children live in areas that are nearly inaccessible. Volunteers travel by boat, bicycle, and even on foot, carrying cold-storage boxes of polio vaccine. In war-torn regions, armed guards are sometimes necessary. One vaccinator in Somalia was killed by a crocodile!

A big obstacle to eradication is fear. Untrue rumors that the polio vaccine contained the AIDS virus or that the vaccine would leave girls unable to have children caused many parents in India and Nigeria to refuse vaccination for their children. Even one unvaccinated child makes it possible for polio to spread.

In 2001, three of the necessary rounds of vaccine had been given in Afghanistan. The fourth and final doses were scheduled for November. Then the terrorist attacks of September 11 occurred, and by the time the vaccines were due, fighting between the Al Qaeda and U.S.-led coalition forces was at its peak. Thousands of people had fled Afghanistan to different areas.

While bombers flew overhead, the courageous volunteers and staff spent three dangerous days administering polio vaccine. More than five million Afghan children were immunized.

No one should have to suffer from a disease that has been preventable for more than half a century. Originally, 2000 was the target date for the world to be polio-free. Although that goal was not met, we are getting closer. Someday soon I hope I can say these words: There is no more polio. *There is no more polio!*

Special Thanks

My thanks to Renée Anderson and Dorothy Bremer, my hospital roommates, who dug into their memories for specific incidents and into their closets for old photographs and other memorabilia. Some of the pictures in this book are here because Renée and Dorothy so graciously shared them. Renée even saved some issues of the *Clutch*, our hospital newsletter, which helped enormously to jog my memory.

The photos of my parents and my brother are courtesy of my mother, Elizabeth Schulze. Her memories also helped.

Mary Beth Lamb, M.D., and Mark Levy, M.D., cheerfully answered my medical questions. I am grateful for their expert help and their friendship.

The King County, Washington, public libraries always come through for me. When I ask questions such as, "What time was the 'Lone Ranger' broadcast on the radio in Minneapolis in 1949?" the staff is happy to help me find out.

Richard R. Owen, M.D., retired medical director, Sister Kenny Institute, Minneapolis, helped me find my old hospital records. Joan L. Headley, executive director, International Polio Network, St. Louis, also helped me find the information I needed.

My agent, Emilie Jacobson of Curtis Brown, Ltd., gave me confidence and encouragement. My editor, Abby Levine, offered thoughtful and skilled suggestions which greatly improved my original manuscript.

Last, thank you to the many students in schools where I've talked who, upon learning I once had polio, asked me to write a book about it. Here it is; I hope you like it.

Books for Young People
by Peg Kehret

Abduction!

Cages

Danger at the Fair

Deadly Stranger

Don't Tell Anyone

Earthquake Terror

Escaping the Giant Wave

Five Pages a Day: A Writer's Journey

The Ghost's Grave

The Hideout

Horror at the Haunted House

I'm Not Who You Think I Am

My Brother Made Me Do It

Night of Fear

Nightmare Mountain

The Richest Kids in Town

Saving Lilly

Searching for Candlestick Park
The Secret Journey
Shelter Dogs: Amazing Stories of Adopted Strays
Sisters, Long Ago
Small Steps: The Year I Got Polio
Spy Cat
The Stranger Next Door
Terror at the Zoo
Trapped
The Winner

The Blizzard Disaster
The Flood Disaster
The Volcano Disaster

Acting Natural
Encore: More Winning Monologs for Young Actors
Winning Monologs for Young Actors

The Frightmares Series:

#1: Cat Burglar on the Prowl

#2: Bone Breath and the Vandals

#3: Don't Go Near Mrs. Tallie

#4: Desert Danger

#5: The Ghost Followed Us Home

#6: Race to Disaster

#7: Screaming Eagles

#8: Backstage Fright

A DVD, "A Visit with Peg Kehret," is available from Best Day Ever Video Productions, 17116 N.E. 5th Place, Bellevue, WA 98008 (www.bestdayevervideo.com).

You can learn more about Peg Kehret at her web site, www.pegkehret.com.

Bibliography

Black, Kathryn. *In the Shadow of Polio*. Boston: Addison-Wesley, 1996.

Bruno, Richard L. *The Polio Paradox*. New York: Warner Books, 2002.

Cohn, Victor. *Sister Kenny: The Woman Who Challenged the Doctors*. Minneapolis: University of Minnesota Press, 1975.

Kenny, Elizabeth, with Martha Ostenso. *And They Shall Walk*. New York: Dodd, Mead, 1943.

Kluger, Jeffrey. *Splendid Solution: Jonas Salk and the Conquest of Polio*. New York: G. P. Putnam's Sons, 2004.

Oshinsky, David M. *Polio: An American Story*. New York: Oxford University Press, 2005.

Paul, John R. *A History of Poliomyelitis*. New Haven:
    Yale University Press, 1971.

Salgado, Sebastiao. *The End of Polio: A Global Effort to End
    a Disease*. New York: Bulfinch Press, AOL Time
    Warner Book Group, 2003.

Seavey, Nina Gilden, Jane S. Smith, and Paul Wagner.
    A Paralyzing Fear: The Triumph Over Polio in America.
    New York: TV Books, 1998.

Silver, Julie K., M.D. *Post-Polio Syndrome: A Guide for
    Polio Survivors and Their Families*. New Haven and
    London: Yale University Press, 2001.

Smith, Jane S. *Patenting the Sun: Polio and the Salk Vaccine*.
    New York: William Morrow, 1990.

Sterling, Dorothy, and Philip Sterling. *Polio Pioneers*.
    Garden City, N.Y.: Doubleday, 1955.